ART DECO KNITS

CREATING A HAND-KNIT WARDROBE
INSPIRED BY THE 1920s–1930s

ART DECO KNITS

CREATING A HAND-KNIT WARDROBE
INSPIRED BY THE 1920s–1930s

JEMIMA BICKNELL

THE CROWOOD PRESS

First published in 2019 by
The Crowood Press Ltd
Ramsbury, Marlborough
Wiltshire SN8 2HR

www.crowood.com

British Library Cataloguing-in-Publication Data
A catalogue record for this book is available from the British Library.

ISBN 978 1 78500 549 7

Typeset by Sharon Dainton.
Printed and bound in India by Parksons Graphics.

CONTENTS

ACKNOWLEDGEMENTS

I am so grateful to the many people who helped to bring this book into existence, both directly and indirectly. Firstly, special thanks are due to three amazing women: Rachel Atkinson, Susan Cropper and Juju Vail. To Juju, without whom this book would not have happened, to Rachel, who showed me a career with sticks and string was possible, and to Susan, for offering me my very first job in this knitting business – thank you so much. Thank you also to the Loopettes (and Loop Lad!), past and present, and to all of my knitting friends and colleagues. I couldn't have done this without your support over the years.

Thank you also to my technical editor, Laura Chau, for her eagle eye and careful pattern checking, and to my wonderful mother-in-law, Kate Stanley, for providing her family photographs for this book.

More thanks are due to my husband than is possible to express here. He has worn many hats during the creation of this book – photographer, proof reader, therapist – and I am so grateful.

Finally, I'd like to dedicate this book to my knitting partner-in-crime and my number one cheerleader – Mum, this book is for you. I hope you like it!

INTRODUCTION

No other era captures our imagination quite like the 'Jazz Age'. Nearly every generation has reinterpreted the era's style, fashion and mood in some way, and creators in all areas of design return to it again and again, drawing fresh inspiration each time. Art Deco, the wide-ranging style that left its mark on everything from architecture to fashion, is continually appealing. Decorative, but not fussy, clean, but not boring, Art Deco design was wildly popular during the inter-war period and continues to be drawn upon today.

For those creators interested in making beautiful clothing for their own wardrobe, the 1920s and 30s can be a particularly inspiring period, as it marks the beginning of fashion as a desirable and accessible pastime, no longer limited to the richest section of society. Cultural change shapes fashion, and few periods contained as much cultural, social and economic change as the two decades between the First and Second World Wars. The clothes women wore represented (and sometimes asserted) their increasing social freedoms, including the growing acceptance of female suffrage and greater (albeit still limited) opportunities for women to earn an income. Clothes could now 'make the woman' and an increasing supply of sewing and knitting patterns meant that women could now make the clothes – not just as a practical fulfilment of domestic requirements, but also as a source of joy and self-expression.

This book aims to encourage this joy and self-expression in the modern knitter who is drawn to the glitter of the 1920s and the elegance of the 1930s. It is split into three parts. The first section, 'Style and Materials', introduces the fashionable silhouettes and design details of the 1920s and 30s, and shows how they were interpreted in the knitting patterns of the period. This section also gives helpful information on the basics of a successful knitting project, including tools, materials, how to read your knitting and the importance of tension. The second section, 'Techniques', covers everything you need to know to create beautifully patterned and embellished fabrics, and includes a stitch dictionary of Art Deco-inspired stitch patterns. Finally, there are nine patterns inspired by various aspects of the period. These patterns are designed as a starting point for your own creativity, and each includes ideas and tips for tweaking them to create your own unique projects and, ultimately, build your own vintage-inspired wardrobe.

CHAPTER 1

THE 1920s - BRIGHT YOUNG THINGS

The silhouette of the 1920s woman is instantly recognizable. Ask someone to describe her and the 'flapper' will quickly come to mind, a wild party girl wearing a loose, fringed evening dress and long strands of pearls, with bobbed hair and a cloche hat completing the look. The flapper girl is certainly an important and enduring facet of the 1920s look but the classic style did not appear immediately and throughout the decade fashionable silhouettes morphed and changed to reflect the cultural developments of the time. This variety is helpful to keep in mind when we are looking to the 1920s for inspiration as specific design details from the period can be adjusted to suit your body shape, while still maintaining an overall vintage look. There was more to 1920s clothing than shift dresses and fringe!

The straighter, simplified look that we associate with the 1920s actually had its roots in the Edwardian period. The silhouette had already begun to loosen over the course of the 1910s, in part due to the new physically demanding roles filled by women during the First World War. Corsets – at least the rigid, whale-bone enforced kind, as fashion had by no

means finished with the use of underwear to shape the female body – had already started to fall out of favour as freedom of movement and comfort became more of a concern to the fashionable woman.

As the decade began, dresses became loose and shift-like and the waist began to drop lower on the body, towards the hip. The general silhouette was intended to be long, lean and tubular in appearance, giving the wearer a boyish look without visible curves. These slim lines were encouraged with elasticated undergarments – the (slightly!) more comfortable successor to the corset. For the first time in history, hemlines began to creep upwards – reaching calf-length in the first half of the decade and eventually rising all the way up to the knee. Although relatively demure by today's standards, this was a radical departure from Victorian concern over visible ankles from only a few decades earlier! Sport and leisure activities such as golfing and tennis were increasingly popular, and these energetic new pastimes required comfortable clothing that allowed for easy movement.

This simplification of the silhouette introduced 'fashion' to

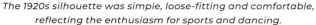

The 1920s silhouette was simple, loose-fitting and comfortable, reflecting the enthusiasm for sports and dancing.

For the 1920s woman, a slim, boyish shape was preferred, with curves suppressed as much as possible. Deep V-necks and horizontal bands at the hip accentuated the tubular look.

a far wider audience than ever before. In contrast to the careful fitting and complex construction of garments in previous decades, a fashionable dress now consisted of only a few pattern pieces, required simple fitting techniques, and could easily be sewn by the enterprising home seamstress in an evening. Fashion and style were now accessible, desirable, and within reach, a development that went hand in hand with the growth of the glamorous new world of Hollywood and cinema. The 'silver screen' offered plenty of fashionable inspi-

ration and women could emulate the wardrobe of their favourite actress relatively easily.

Of course, while the basic silhouette was simple, the fashionable wardrobe of the 1920s was certainly not plain. A minimalistic shape allowed for a greater focus on design details at the hip, hem and neck or shoulder, which were often emphasized with pleated or gathered fabric, artificial flowers, and embroidery. Unusual collars or necklines were also common and featured bows, cut-out effects or contrasting colour details. Sleeves were usually either slim fitting, or loose and gathered into tight cuffs at the wrist. Design details might also be placed at the cuffs with beading, buttons or embroidery. Further interest could be added to the basic garment shape by dividing it up into sections with horizontal stripes, bands of pattern or sections of embroidery. These bands of embellishment would sit low on the hip or at the hem of the garment to emphasize the straight lines of the torso and skirt.

Evening wear also featured a loose, straight silhouette, but reworked in the most luxurious of fabrics. These dresses could have exquisite embellishment, with dense beadwork and embroidery adding interest to the clean lines of draped and pleated fabric. However, the new dance crazes required that evening dress be practical as well as beautiful, allowing plenty of room for movement – arms were often left entirely bare and dresses could be cut very low at the back. They were short, falling to the calf or knee, and many featured surprisingly modern-looking uneven hemlines with shorter skirts at the front or sides. Evening dresses might also have more fullness at the hem than day wear. This was particularly true in the second half of the decade, when ruffles and panels of extra fabric were added to the lower part of the skirt, often asymmetrically. Shoulders could also be asymmetrical, with a single shoulder emphasized with large bows, flowers or lengths of draped fabric. Beaded overlays were loosely attached over the main fabric and tassels or long lengths of fringe might be sewn at the hip. These tactile, textured embellishments were perfectly designed to catch the light as the wearer danced the night away.

Accessories

Few items are as potent a reflection of the 1920s as the cloche hat. Equal parts elegant and rebellious, these stylish hats were worn pulled down low on the forehead, shading the eyes and framing the face, and are an iconic feature of the decade's fashion. Hats were an important part of the fashionable lady's wardrobe and were often made eye-catching through the use of intricate design details such as ribbons, bows and trims. Hats might be in a neutral colour and an interesting shape, designed to be worn with several different outfits. It was also common in more fashionable circles to match the hat to the garment. Cloche hats could vary considerably in design – the brim might be worn turned up at the front or side, the crown

1920s silhouettes at a glance

- Loose-fitting skirts or dresses with a calf- or knee-length hemline

- Either no waist (shift dresses) or a dropped waist, pulled in at the mid- or upper-hip

- Narrow, close-fitting sleeves, or draped and gathered at the wrist

- Embellishment details placed at the hip, neckline and shoulders, including sash belts or unusually shaped collars

- Pleated, gathered or draped fabric

- Sportswear influence

- Outerwear trimmed with fur

Accessories were an important part of the 1920s wardrobe. Close-fitting cloche hats framed the face and brightly patterned scarves would add colour to a practical outfit.

could be rounded, fitted closely to the head, or large and angular. Wide-brimmed hats were also worn, although these were less common. More exotic styles of headwear appeared for evening wear, with jewelled turbans or headbands becoming popular. Long, thin scarves might be tied around the head, either over a hat or alone, with the ends tied in a bow or allowed to fall down the back.

Scarves and shawls were hugely versatile and could be worn in many different ways. Small neck scarves might be tied tightly around the neck beneath a matching cloche hat. Alternatively, scarves might be tied in a bow beneath a large collar or added to the front of a dress to soften a neckline. Sometimes scarves and shawls would be integrated completely into an outfit. Large plain or embellished shawls might be tied as a sash around the hips to shape a dress, or long scarves could be attached to one shoulder and wound once about the neck before joining the draped fabric of the dress, falling in soft folds to the hem. Scarves and shawls might be carefully matched to an outfit or worn in a bright contrasting colour with a black or neutral-coloured garment. Thick fur stoles, cuffs and collars were also popular.

Gloves and cuffs were worn for practical reasons and as extra decoration. Leather gloves were common for day wear,

particularly with the increase in leisure activities and interest in driving. For evening, bare arms would be complemented by short, detached cuffs in a delicate fabric, often alongside jewelled bangles and armbands. The look could be completed with a small beaded evening bag.

Fabrics and Colours

Thanks to the colourful art movements of the previous two decades, bright colours were already being used for fashionable wear by the 1920s. High-end evening wear could be particularly vivid and featured a wide range of bright jewel shades. Very fashionable day dresses might also be colourful, but muted or neutral fabrics were generally more common for day wear. For women with lower incomes, day dresses tended to be worn in darker shades and lifted with brightly coloured accessories. Black was popular and worked particularly well for evening when embroidered with gold and silver thread and beads. Black was also frequently used as part of bold colour combinations and might be paired with bright pink or red.

Garments and accessories would often be worn together in a single matching shade, with particular design details picked out in a contrast colour or fabric. Sportswear influences manifested in crisp white fabrics with bright trims. Although less common than solid colours, prints were also used for day wear and were usually bold, graphic and slightly abstract. Stripes and plaid patterns might also be used.

In high-end fashion, the fabric itself would often be the primary focus of the outfit. Combining simple shapes with heavily beaded and embroidered fabrics, designers would draw on Art Deco influences and cover dresses with embroidered fish scales, feathers, angular linework, and stylized floral motifs. Whether through printed patterns or embellishment, fabrics often reflected the fashionable preoccupation with 'Orientalism' – a kind of romanticized, fantastical exoticism that drew on sources as varying as Russian embroidery and Ancient Egyptian hieroglyphs.

Luxurious fabrics such as silk, velvet and shiny metallic lamé tended to be used for high-end evening wear, with jersey, crepe and rayon (the emerging 'artificial silk') worn during the day. Drape was of paramount importance for both day and evening fabrics, in order to achieve the desired silhouette. A simple design could be enhanced through the use of con-

---

1920s accessories at a glance

- Close-fitting cloche hats, plain or embellished with ribbon

- Silk neck scarves tied closely around the neck or head

- Large scarves tied under the collar or wrapped around the neck

- Short close-fitting gloves for day wear

- Detached cuffs in delicate and embellished fabrics

- Fur stoles and collars

- Small beaded evening bags

trasting fabrics, with pieces of matte and shiny fabrics placed together on the diagonal or thick stripes of print alternated with a solid colour. Evening dress featured similar contrasts, with fine translucent voile sleeves ending in solid fabric cuffs. Fur gave a luxurious texture and was used to trim the hems and cuffs of both dresses and outerwear or worn as thick collars and stoles.

1920s fabrics at a glance

- Solid colours with contrasting colour or print design details

- Luxurious silk, velvet and lame fabrics for evening

- Jersey and crepe fabrics for day wear

- Comfortable fabrics with excellent drape

- Bold, abstract and stylized prints

- Heavily embellished fabrics with intricate embroidery and beadwork

- Contrasting textures and finishes

- Black or bright jewel shades for evening

- Neutrals and muted shades for day wear

This mid-1920s outfit combined a bold pattern with a solid colour. Fun square buttons added extra decoration.

CHAPTER 2

THE 1930s – EMERGING ELEGANCE

In terms of garment shapes, the 1930s can be a much more approachable style to incorporate into the modern knitter's wardrobe than the 1920s. As the decade progressed, waistlines returned to their natural position on the body, trousers were introduced into women's wardrobes, and the production of knitting patterns exploded. Although in some ways the 1930s can seem a quite conservative time in fashion (especially when compared to the rapid changes in culture and fashion seen in the previous decade), the blend of simple, flattering shapes and innovative detail is both inspirational and wearable. When looking at the 1930s silhouette, you can see that the flapper girl of the 1920s had 'grown up' into a sophisticated and elegant woman and her wardrobe had matured to match.

The 1920s had been all about the straight silhouette: shift dresses, boyish figures, and very few curves. However, as the decade came to a close, waistlines had already begun to rise again. A slim, defined waist at the natural waistline soon became a feature of the 1930s silhouette and this shape has seldom been completely out of fashion since. Many sweaters

were neatly fitted at the waist and were fairly cropped, making them a perfect match for high-waisted slacks and skirts. In the early part of the 1930s, garments were still worn loose around the bust, giving a bloused effect above the close-fitting waist. This silhouette bridged the gap between the loose, relaxed shapes of the 1920s and the more tailored looks that would begin to appear in the later part of the decade and into the 1940s. Longer blouses, sweaters and dresses were also worn, but these might be belted to further emphasize the waist and give a neat, close-fitting shape.

The return to feminine curves reflected a general shift towards prettiness in fashion, with bows, ruffles and flowers becoming more common in both day and evening wear. Hemlines dropped again, returning to calf length for day wear, and skirts often featured inset panels and gathering or pleating towards the hem. Although trousers were worn, they were usually cut very loose and maintained the softly feminine silhouette. Greater emphasis began to be given to the shoulders, with puffed sleeves, ruffles and even oversized 'leg-of-mutton' sleeves becoming common as the decade the upper shoulders. Lower necklines could be square-cut, V-necked or draped in a soft cowl, and might be emphasized with embroidery, bows and ruffles. Cuffs were often also emphasized and might be worked to match a brightly coloured collar on an otherwise plain dress.

For evening wear, elegance was key. Dresses were cut on the bias, creating a beautiful draped column of fabric that fell all the way to the floor and gracefully skimmed the body. The front neck might have a loosely draped cowl neckline, or it might be cut high with a dramatically low back. Strands of diamante might be added across the back for a touch of sparkle. These simple dresses were not necessarily plain – printed fabric began to be used for evening wear as well as day wear during the decade – but they were usually less embellished than the party dresses of the 1920s had been, with an emphasis on cut and drape rather than beadwork and embroidery. Although arms were sometimes left bare, interesting sleeve shapes also began to appear in evening wear. Sleeves were sometimes even detached from the dress, worn separately on the upper arm and leaving the shoulder bare. Small matching capes might be worn over dresses, covering the shoulders and featuring fur- or diamante-trimmed collars.

progressed. The use of boleros or short jackets layered over the shoulders and bust further emphasized the top part of the torso. Alternatively, the shoulders might be slim and close fitting with large bell sleeves gathered into a tight cuff.

Necklines became even more varied, with a huge range of different shapes available. Blouses could be high-necked, with small, neat collars or large lacy fichus that lay like capes over

Prettiness and femininity reappeared in the 1930s with delicate florals, puffed sleeves and small decorative bows.

No longer hidden beneath boxy shift dresses, women's waists could be accentuated with deep sections of rib. Necklines were interesting and feminine with large bows or collars.

Garments might be sleek and close fitting in the body, with large statement sleeves and eye-catching diamante fastenings for a glamorous evening look.

A belt could be added in a matching or contrast fabric to accentuate the waist on longer sweaters.

Accessories

During the 1930s accessories became even more varied and widely worn. With the recent recession making it difficult to afford the latest fashions, fashionable women could update their look much more economically by adding a new hat or scarf. Accessories were increasingly bright, fun and feminine and could be mixed and matched easily to create new outfits. Cloche hats continued to be popular, although the brim now lifted slightly further away from the face and was often folded up at the top or the side to reveal the forehead. Some hats were very small and performed a purely decorative function – they could be worn at a jaunty angle on one side of the head, allowing the wearer to properly display their perfectly finger-waved hairstyle on the other. These small hats would often feature embellishments such as ribbons, feathers and artificial flowers. Turban-style hats continued to be worn and smart little knitted or felt berets were popular. For the brave trend-setter, increasingly interesting (and perhaps, for some, slightly difficult to wear!) hat shapes appeared, with pointed crowns decorated with buttons and tassels. Hats might also have a small lace veil attached to them to cover the eyes.

Gloves became increasingly popular during the 1930s. During the day, short leather or fabric gloves would be worn, sometimes with decoration at the cuff. Gloves were now also worn with evening wear. These tended to be long, reaching

Hats became increasingly fun and varied in shape and were worn at a flattering angle. Thick fur collars and cuffs added a luxurious finishing touch.

Fabrics and Colours

The new appetite for prettiness was reflected in the colours and fabrics of the 1930s wardrobe. Pale pastels and muted shades remained popular, but many bright shades were now worn in both day and evening wear. Colour combinations could be bold and unexpected, with several primary colours combined in single garments. Black continued to be considered very chic and would be accessorized with pops of bright colour. Prints became very popular and were used in evening wear as well as day wear, replacing the expensive, heavily embellished fabrics of the 1920s. Prints could be large and bold or small, delicate and floral, reflecting the new feminine aesthetic. Stripes and plaid patterns continued to be popular and were joined by fun dotted prints.

Increasingly successful artificial imitations of luxe fabrics appeared, replacing the expensive embellished fabrics that

to the elbow or beyond, although short lace gloves might also be seen. Long cuffs (what modern knitters might call wrist warmers) were also worn on the forearms, usually in a delicate or embellished fabric that complemented the fabric of the gown.

As in the 1920s, scarves were frequently incorporated into an outfit. Silk scarves might be tied under a neat collar, or a longer sash could be wrapped around the waist to create the fashionable nipped-in shape. Scarves could be bright and cheerful and might match the hat for a coordinated set. Fur continued to be a very popular accessory for both evening and day wear and was used as a trim along cuffs, collars and hems, as well as for luxurious stoles.

Prints began to be used for evening wear, trimmed with bands of contrasting fabric. Evening dresses were long, with a simple silhouette and a focus on elegant cut and drape.

few could now afford. The growing popularity of 'art silk' (rayon), alongside the simplicity of the new evening wear fashions, meant that glamour was now accessible to a much wider audience and no longer required a large income. Embellishment did not disappear completely though, and very high-end designs could feature sparkling diamante trims. Fur was also extremely popular as a trim, with cheaper varieties available as well as faux fur made from cotton pile.

CHAPTER 3

HAND-KNITTING IN THE 1920s AND 30s

Knitting in the 1920s

Great inspiration is to be found in this period for the modern maker, as it marks the beginning of self-made fashion. Before the 1920s, hand-knitting had been primarily a practical matter, with knitters producing vests, socks and other plain underwear items for their family. Knitting had been especially important during the First World War, when producing hardwearing knitted items for soldiers was both a necessity and a way to show love and support for the men away from home. Once the war was over, it would be understandable if this impressive production line of practical knitwear might have led to something of an ennui for hand-knitting. However, as the 1920s progressed and a greater variety of patterns and yarn began to appear, enthusiasm for the craft continued to grow.

Accessible Style

During the 1920s, home sewing machines and cheap printed knitting and sewing patterns became increasingly available. These new patterns often came as part of women's magazines such as *Woman's Weekly* and *Woman and Home* and brought the new fashions to the ordinary woman. Fashion was now accessible to many more people and couture looks could be emulated by those who could never dream of affording the originals.

This new interest in home-made fashion was helped by the simplicity of the new styles. The knitting patterns of the early 1920s followed the fashionable straight silhouette and were often tubular, loose, and involved little to no shaping. Instead, drawstrings might be used to draw the sweater in above the hips or around the neck. They were also generally worked in simple stitches such as stocking stitch, with perhaps some crochet or lace added at the hips or the neck for interest, and were often marketed for their simplicity and approachability,

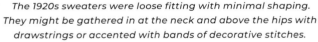

The 1920s sweaters were loose fitting with minimal shaping. They might be gathered in at the neck and above the hips with drawstrings or accented with bands of decorative stitches.

Simple shapes and stitches would be embellished with touches of embroidery at the neckline or lacy patterns at the hip.

assuring the aspirational 'bright young thing' that a fashionable sweater could be worked in one piece, and made in a day.

Fashionable practicality

As the 1920s progressed, the sweaters became longer, with the hem reaching the hip or below. This tubular knitted look was enhanced further as sweater suits became popular, with skirts and sweaters knitted to match each other and create a long line. Maintaining this fashionably clean silhouette

remained an important aspect of knitting pattern design. In a 1928 issue of *Woman and Home*, 'A Pull-over of Good Line' was proclaimed to keep a 'Smart Silhouette when the Wearer is in Motion as well as when she is in Repose', a selling point that was particularly important considering the new active hobbies women were engaging in. Many knitting patterns were inspired by the new vogue for sports such as golf and tennis, as knitted fabric allowed a much more practical range of motion than woven garments. The practical and beautiful features of knitted fabric were also now fully recognized by couture designers, most notably by Chanel, whose use of jersey in her 1916 collection helped to place knitted fabric firmly on the fashion map. The endorsement of knitwear by the trendsetters of the day encouraged an increasing appetite for new patterns; knitters began to value the most up-to-date trends and styles over the practical items that had previously been the focus of pattern leaflets and magazines.

The confident knitter

The increasing desire for knitwear – and the confidence of knitters in replicating new styles – led to a greater variation in pattern as the decade progressed. Although the fashionable shape remained simple throughout the 1920s, touches of embellishment began to be introduced and patterns became more complex. Horizontal contrasting bands appeared in many knitwear designs, either through thick two-colour stripes at the hips, or sections of more complex lace or textured stitch patterns. Thick bands of ribbing at the hem of long sweaters would cling to the hips, leaving the waist loose. Embroidery was also common, either as a simple motif added to a pocket or more complex designs worked along button bands and necklines and above ribbed sections at the hip. A great deal of care and enthusiasm can be clearly seen in these new designs and women were eager to embrace this ability to create something fashionable and unique.

A craze for colourwork

Part of this growing confidence was reflected in the new enthusiasm for colourwork, particularly Fair Isle patterns from Shetland. The starting point for this craze (and possibly the resurgence of fashionable knitting in general) is often credited to the Prince of Wales, who was pictured wearing a Fair Isle sweater in 1921. This royal endorsement from a fashion icon caused a surge in popularity for knitted garments from Shetland, which ticked many of fashionable boxes for the 1920s woman: a loose, androgynous fit, bright and colourful patterns, and an energetic 'sporty' air (Fair Isle sweaters and vests were often worn while golfing).

Knitting in the 1930s

The economic crash in 1929 did nothing to slow down the popularity for hand-knitting – if anything, knitting and home dressmaking became even more popular during the 1930s as it allowed some distraction and control in an uncertain and difficult time. Patterns continued to offer access to the world of fashion and gave knitters a cheap way to whip up a new outfit.

Changing silhouettes

As the fashionable silhouette started to shift, knitting patterns quickly began to reflect the new shape. Sweaters became shorter, with hems creeping up to sit at the high hip. New designs were given a close-fitting shape through the waist with a deep section of rib before blousing into a loose fit around the bust. A greater variation in silhouette and style also began to appear. Whereas the fashionable shape of the 1920s had been fairly stable and ubiquitous – simple, straight, tubular, with as few curves as possible – the 1930s had a variety of different silhouettes depending on the preferences of the knitter. The new sweaters might be extra-feminine, with

Designs became increasingly challenging as knitters sought new and interesting patterns. This cardigan features a diamond lace panel, lines of delicate rope cables and a neat folded collar.

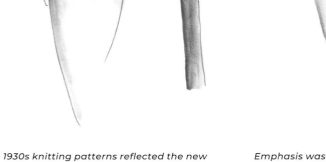

1930s knitting patterns reflected the new feminine aesthetic with all-over lace patterns and the addition of ruffles and frills at the neck and cuffs.

Emphasis was placed on the shoulders through the addition of large, cape-like collars and puffed sleeves. Party sweaters would be worn with sparkling brooches or sweater clips for extra glamour.

Silhouettes could also be sleek and tailored, particularly towards the end of the 1930s. Rib and other textured stitches would be used to create a slim fit in the body and sleeves.

large frills at the neck and lacy all-over stitch patterns. Or they might be neat and close fitting, with a simple knit-purl stitch pattern and a tailored look. Sleeves and collars could be distinctive and oversized, or smart and subtle. The explosion of innovative designs and styles over this period turned knitting into a fun, easy and empowering way to express oneself – a feeling that is easily recognizable to the modern knitter.

A return to prettiness

As the silhouette became more feminine, emphasis shifted away from simplicity and ease of motion, towards prettiness. The loose, bloused silhouette gave a romantic feel and would

sometimes be enhanced with long ties at the waist for a wrapped look. Sleeves were gathered into large puffed sleeves at the cap and upper arm, emphasizing the contrast with the newly emerged waist. Alternatively, sleeves might be loose and gathered at the elbow for a bell-shaped effect. Delicate, feminine knitted fabrics were used to complement the new womanly shape, with lacy stitch patterns appearing around the neck, or as an all-over pattern. Embellishments became much more pronounced – ruffles and frills were common additions to the hems, sleeves and necklines of sweaters, as well as knitted and crocheted flowers and bows. Embroidery continued to appear as a floral touch to finished jumpers throughout the decade.

Decorative scarves and cowls could be worked separately and worn as part of a coordinated outfit or integrated into the garment itself. They might be worked in a matching colour or using bright contrasting shades.

lored look would begin to extend into the sleeves, with angular sleeve caps appearing and emphasizing the shoulder line.

Challenging design

Patterns continued to become more complex, worked in multiple pieces and requiring a greater level of finishing skill. Knitwear could now be the focus of a fashionable outfit, aiming to be both interesting to knit and eye-catching to wear. Designs became increasingly daring and ambitious. New patterns might include large cowl-shaped necklines, created with interesting shaping or through the addition of a separate knitted piece. Some designs would have removable scarves in knitted or woven fabrics incorporated into the neckline, allowing the sweater to be worn in multiple ways and altered according to the wearer's mood. The thriftiness of a versatile sweater design was a common selling point: a single pattern would often have several pictured variations, giving a couple of different options for cuffs and collars.

The neckline was frequently the focus for this innovation in design, with a wide variety of collar styles appearing in knitting patterns. Collars might be oversized in a contrasting colour or stitch pattern, lying flat across the shoulders and pulled together at the throat with a brooch or large button. Sometimes this style of collar was so large it became a small cape, sitting over the entire upper bust and often worked in a pretty lace stitch or with a delicate edging. Other collars might be folded or gathered, or extend into long ends that could be tied in a bow at the neck.

Smart and tailored

Alongside the new trend for prettiness, a smart, tailored look was also popular. This was characterized by a close-fitting silhouette and an emphasis on line-based – rather than lacy – stitch patterns. The neck was often high with a neat button placket at the front or back neck for ease of wear, or it might have a smart shirt-style collar. The sleeves were usually narrow, and the sweater might be belted above the ribbing to emphasize the waist. Design interest would come from simple knit and purl stitch patterns, angular eyelet details, or from the use of contrasting colours for different sections of the design. Later in the decade, as the 1940s approached, this tai-

A sweater for every mood

One of the most charming aspects of knitwear from this period is the way new patterns were marketed to the enthusiastic knitter. Knitted garments were not simply a practical way of keeping warm – instead, they were very much tied to a mood or an activity, often with an aspirational or uplifting message attached. A sweater might be advertised as 'charming', or 'perfect for parties', for example. Or, for the sporty modern woman, a sweater specifically designed for golf or tennis might be suggested. Choosing the perfect new project might be almost as fun as the knitting, with pattern browsing, selection, planning and daydreaming all becoming part of the process – a process that will be familiar to many modern knitters.

CHAPTER 4

VINTAGE STYLE FOR THE MODERN KNITTER

The previous chapters covered the silhouettes, the fabrics, the shapes and design details of the 1920s and 30s – but how do you incorporate them into your knitted wardrobe without feeling as though you are in costume? This might be a daunting prospect and it can be difficult to know where to start, especially if this is your first time experimenting with vintage style. However, there are many different ways to add a subtle Art Deco flair to your knitting and it's easy to adapt these influences to suit your comfort, style and body shape.

Dipping into Deco

One of the easiest ways to experiment with style from this period is to look at the fabrics and embellishments used, rather than shapes and silhouettes. Art Deco-style motifs and stitch patterns can be very effective and it's easy to incorporate them into 'modern' accessories. Start with a basic wrist warmer or fingerless glove pattern – the Becket mitts would work well – and experiment with adding some embroidery or a bead pattern to the back of the hand. The small scale of the project keeps the pressure down and fingerless gloves can fit easily into a modern or vintage outfit. For a larger scale project, a scarf or rectangular shawl worked in an Art Deco cable pattern is perfect for throwing over a modern coat, especially when worked in a slightly thicker yarn. Classic garment shapes are timeless and provide a blank canvas on which to apply as much as or little design detail as you like – try adding a decorative panel to a simple sweater for a subtle look or embellish the cuffs and collar with some Art Deco-inspired embroidery.

Experiment with silhouette

There's a reason it was fashionable to be very slim in the 1920s – the dropped waist silhouette is not the easiest style to wear for many women! However, with a bit of experimentation it's perfectly possible to adjust this shape to flatter your figure while maintaining a silhouette that nods to the period.

Shawls are an easy way to experiment with Art Deco-inspired stitch patterns. Keep the look relaxed and modern by wearing them casually wrapped around the neck like a scarf.

If you're working with beads for the first time, start off with a small project like fingerless mitts and work a beaded pattern around the cuff. Just a few beads can turn a plain project into something unique.

Choose a loose-fitting sweater design with no (or minimal) waist shaping but keep it slightly shorter than an authentic 1920s shift sweater would be, with the hem hitting the high hip instead of mid or lower hip. Adding some beaded decoration in bands at the hem can give a further touch of Art Deco even if the shape has been adjusted. Even a very cropped sweater can have a 1920s feel when worked in a yarn with shine and drape, especially when combined with an Art Deco-inspired stitch pattern. Just make sure the overall shape stays relaxed, loose and comfortable, as this was the primary style of the 1920s.

For a sleeker style, the silhouette of the 1930s can be more approachable and is usually easy to wear. For a very simple version of the look, choose sweaters that are fairly close fitting, slightly cropped and with a deep rib at the waist. Alternatively, a longer slim-fitting sweater can be worn, with a belt emphasizing the waist. If you're feeling brave, draw attention to the shoulders with puffed sleeve caps or ruffles at the neck and shoulders.

Mix and match with modern

Vintage-inspired pieces can blend in perfectly with modern pieces, so don't be afraid to mix and match. A relaxed 1920s-style sweater can work brilliantly over skinny jeans, as the sleek lines of the lower half balance out the loose silhouette of the top. Alternatively, combine a smart pencil skirt with a fitted sweater for an office-appropriate outfit with a 1930s feel. Look out for clothing and accessories to combine with your knitwear for a vintage look – a striking pair of earrings could play on the Art Deco lines of a sweater, or a classic cardigan can be layered over a pussy-bow blouse.

Knitted accessories are particularly easy to add to modern outfits and are the perfect opportunity to allow your creativity to run wild when practising beading, embroidery and new stitch patterns.

Finding knitting patterns

A wider range of knitting patterns is available now than ever before. Plenty of patterns can give a vintage feel or be adapted and tweaked to fit into a vintage wardrobe. Try to see past colour, length and waist shaping, as these are normally easy to adjust. Instead, look out for interesting sleeve shapes and necklines, which are more difficult to recreate. You might also be drawn to a design because of an interesting stitch pattern, or a general silhouette. Spend some time looking at photographs of original knitwear from the period (*see* 'Resources and Further Reading' at the end of this book) as this will help you recognize the key elements of the style when looking at modern patterns. Many original knitting patterns from the period are now available online for a truly authentic knitting experience. The 'language' of knitting patterns has remained generally consistent so you should find them easy to understand. Keep in mind, however, that garments were usually only written for one size and worked in long-since discontinued yarns, so you may need to adjust the pattern considerably to fit.

1920s silhouettes can sometimes feel difficult to wear, so experiment with the length and add some subtle waist shaping if you prefer a more defined look – just keep the overall effect loose fitting and elegant.

The 1930s sweater has a classic fit and a defined waist, making it easy to incorporate into a modern wardrobe. This makes it a great place to start experimenting with vintage silhouettes.

Seek out inspiration

The Art Deco movement itself was incredibly influential — so much so that touches of it can be found almost everywhere once you start looking, from fonts to fashion, architecture to advertisements. This variety of influences provides many rich sources of inspiration for embellishment ideas. Note any motifs or designs that catch your eye and see if you can think of a way to channel them through your knitting, whether it be through stitch pattern, beadwork or embroidery. Look at the work of modern fashion designers and try to spot any vintage-inspired details — seeing how others have been creatively influenced by the 1920s and 30s can be useful when incorporating vintage style into your own wardrobe.

Watching films from the period can also be very helpful and is the best way to see vintage fashions in motion. From the dramatic silent films of the 1920s to the escapism of the 1930s musical, films often featured exquisitely designed Art Deco sets and extravagant costumes that are as awe-inspiring now as they were then. Modern films can also be great sources of inspiration. Although not always completely authentic, seeing how costume designers of each new generation engage with the fashions of the era is fascinating and can encourage you to think creatively.

Fashion in film

From the original 'It' girl herself, Clara Bow, to the fantastical flapper fashion of Chicago, there's a wealth of inspiration to be found on film. These television shows and films feature beautiful costumes and styling – the perfect accompaniment to a vintage-inspired knitting session.

The Great Gatsby (2013)
Singin' in the Rain (1952)
'It' (1927)
Miss Fisher's Murder Mysteries (TV, 2012–2015)
Chicago (2002)
Swing Time (1936)
Midnight in Paris (2011)
42nd Street (1933)
Z: The Beginning of Everything (TV, 2017)
Some Like It Hot (1959)
Agatha Christie's Poirot (1989–2013)

If you're nervous about jumping into a vintage silhouette, try sticking to Art Deco fabrics and mixing them with modern clothing – classic sweaters with Art Deco-inspired cables can look great with jeans.

Keep the vintage influences subtle – simple intersecting lines can give a classic look with a nod to Art Deco design.

CHAPTER 5

BASICS AND MATERIALS

Yarn

It is a wonderful time to be a knitter – the variety of colour, fibre and thickness of yarn available to us today is truly breathtaking, and would no doubt make our vintage counterparts jealous! As yarn is available in a huge range of fibres, a rainbow of colours, and every thickness from the finest cobweb to the chunkiest rope, it can sometimes feel overwhelming trying to choose the right yarn for your project. This section gives a brief introduction to the wide world of yarn and how it relates to creating vintage-inspired knitwear, but there is a huge amount of information available on this topic (*see* 'Resources and Further Reading' at the end of this book).

Yarn weights

Yarns are available in many different thicknesses, or 'weights' and will usually fall into one of the following broad cate-gories. Note that the needle size range given here for each weight is only a guide and the needle size you use for a particular yarn may vary considerably, either to achieve a particular tension or to give the knitted fabric specific properties. For example, a fine yarn might be worked on a relatively large needle to create an open look, or a thicker yarn might be worked tightly on smaller needles for a stiff, structural effect.

Cobweb

Needle size: 2mm or smaller

Sometimes known as 1-ply, cobweb yarns are extremely fine yarns, most often used for heirloom-style lace projects and worked with very fine needles. The resulting fabric is as light as air and extremely intricate patterns can be produced due to the fine gauge. Projects worked in cobweb-weight yarn are certainly not quick knits, but they are a labour of love and can be extremely rewarding to work on.

Yarn is available in a huge range of colours, fibres and thicknesses; 4-ply is a great thickness for working Art Deco-inspired fabrics and patterns as it creates a fine fabric that's sturdy enough to support embellishment.

Lace

Needle size: 2mm–3mm

Lace weight yarns (also referred to as 2-ply yarns) are slightly thicker than cobweb but still very fine and produce a light and delicate fabric. As the name suggests, they are often worked at a fine gauge which allows the creation of intricate lace stitch patterns, although you may also find projects that combine lace weight yarn with large needles for a very open fabric. Lace weight is very popular for lace shawls, but don't be afraid to use it for other accessories or lightweight garments for a spectacular evening look. Lace weight is particular good for fine beadwork, as the yarn is thin enough to pass easily through smaller beads. Extra care should be taken when embroidering

lace weight, however – unless it is worked at a fairly firm gauge, it's easy to pull the delicate fabric out of shape.

4-ply

Needle range: 2.5mm–3.5mm

This is an extremely popular thickness and is the weight used for the majority of projects in this book. It's fine enough to create delicate fabrics and intricate stitch patterns and can be used with relatively small beads, yet is also sturdy enough to hold the weight of beaded and embroidered embellishments. Also called 'fingering' or 'sock' weight, these terms are sometimes used interchangeably, and although they all fall under the 4-ply category you'll find there is considerable variety in the look and feel of 4-ply yarns. Some are very tightly plied (the individual strands that make up the yarn have been twisted more tightly together) and will appear quite fine – these yarns are often fairly hard-wearing, are usually worked at a tighter gauge and are perfect for projects that will see a lot of use, such as mitts or socks. Other 4-ply yarns are more loosely spun and appear more 'plump'. They can be worked at a slightly looser gauge as they will expand to fill the space between stitches, making them a good choice for garments.

Sport

Needle size: 3mm–4mm

A slightly less common thickness, sport weight yarns fall between a 4-ply and DK. If you're looking for a quick knit but still want a fairly 'fine' feel to the fabric, or if you're looking for a particularly 'plump' 4-ply, a sport weight is good choice.

DK

Needle size: 3.5mm–4.5mm

DK (also known as double-knit or 8-ply) weight is a good choice for quick-knit projects without looking too bulky. It will generally be too thick for delicate beadwork, although it can give a lovely dense background for dramatic embroidery motifs and larger beads. The fabric is still fine enough to work special design details such as decorative collars and cuffs and will drape nicely without adding bulk, so it can still give a vintage look. DK weight yarns will also work well with many textural stitch patterns such as larger Deco-inspired cables or strong linework.

The Beckett mitts are worked in a yarn with a small percentage of nylon. Nylon adds strength to other fibres so nylon-blend yarns are perfect for hardwearing projects such as gloves and socks.

Bulky/Chunky
Needle size: 6mm and larger

Very thick yarns were not common during the 1920s and 30s but it's still very possible to use these yarns for an Art Deco-inspired look. A wide scarf worked in a luxuriously thick yarn and fastened with a vintage brooch, for example, can be the perfect winter accessory and will add an elegant finishing touch to an outfit.

Fibre

Yarn is also available in lots of different fibres. Different fibres have different properties and choosing the best one can be the key to a successful project.

Wool

Wool was the most common yarn fibre during the 1920s and 30s and remains very popular among modern knitters. It's comfortable to wear, warm yet breathable, and its elasticity allows wool garments to fit closely to the body and withstand multiple wearings and washings without losing their shape. The texture and feel of wool yarns can vary considerably depending on the sheep breed, with some breeds (such as Merino) being known for their softness and others (such as Wensleydale) for their lustre. Thus, even within the 'wool' category a huge variety of different yarns are available, making it a great all-round choice for accessories and garments.

Silk

Silk yarn has a luxurious sheen and drape, so it works well for glamorous evening garments and shawls. It dyes well, giving a jewel-like colour, and can be very evocative of 1920s decadence. Silk has very little elasticity, so it won't bounce back after blocking. It can work very well for lace shawls as the lace patterns will open up beautifully, but garments worked in 100 per cent silk can stretch out of shape with time. To counteract this, silk is often blended with other fibres such as wool – a good wool-silk blend can strike the perfect balance between luxury and practicality, making it an excellent option for dressier garments.

Worsted
Needle size: 4.5mm–5.5mm

Worsted weight (also known as 10-ply or aran weight, although this is usually on the heavier side) knits up fast so it can be a very tempting option for quick projects. Worsted weight yarns are relatively thick, making very delicate embellishment difficult. Instead, try focusing on the overall silhouette and larger design details when selecting worsted-weight projects to add to your vintage-inspired wardrobe. Alternatively, use a worsted weight yarn for a modern knit with just a touch of vintage inspiration, such as a classic chunky sweater with an Art Deco-inspired Cable Panel.

Cashmere

An extremely soft and fine fibre, 100 per cent cashmere yarn is extra luxurious and often expensive, but can be worth it for a very special finished project. Cashmere is also often blended with silk or wool for added softness.

Angora/Mohair

Angora and mohair yarns are soft, warm and light, and produce a fabric with a lovely soft haze of fibres on the surface. Although angora yarn became increasingly popular during the 1940s and 1950s, it was relatively uncommon in earlier knitting patterns. However, these fluffy yarns are a nice way to add textural variety to your knits and can even give the look of a 'fur' trim – try working the cuffs of a pair of gloves in a fluffy mohair yarn or using a white angora yarn for a luxuriously cosy winter cowl.

Plant fibres

Plant fibres, such as cotton, linen or bamboo, are a lovely option for summer projects. They are cool to wear and usually have excellent drape, making them a good match for loose and relaxed 1920s-style garments.

Acrylic

Acrylic yarn is widely available, inexpensive and hardwearing. It will keep its shape over time and withstand frequent washing, so it's a good choice for projects that will see a lot of use. However, keep in mind that acrylic yarns cannot be opened up with blocking as successfully as natural fibres, so they may not be the best choice for lace stitch patterns. They can also be prone to static, and lower quality acrylic yarns can feel unpleasantly 'squeaky' to work with.

The delicate stitch pattern of the Parelli shawl is perfectly matched with a lace weight blend of wool, silk and yak. Silk adds a glamorous sheen to your projects and has a lovely drape, so it's great for shawls.

Other fibres

Natural fibres are sometimes blended with man-made fibres to give specific properties. For example, a small percentage of nylon will give extra strength to yarns intended for hard-use items like socks. Some yarns also have a strand of glittery thread spun in for extra sparkle, or you can buy a spool of glitter thread separately and hold it together with your working yarn – this can be very effective for evening wear or special occasion projects.

Alpaca

Alpaca yarn was not commonly seen in knitting patterns of the 1920s and 30s, but it is a very popular fibre among modern knitters. It's soft, warm and durable, and can also be a good alternative to sheep wool for those who are allergic to lanolin.

Beads, Buttons and Trims

Adding these embellishments to your knits can turn a plain item into something very special.

Beads

Adding beads to your knitting is easy and satisfying, and the huge variety of colours and finishes available allow for a completely unique final project.

Shape

Rounded seed beads (or rocailles) are the most commonly used beads for knitting, as they fit neatly on the stitch and won't snag your yarn or pull the stitches out of proportion. Other available shapes include cylinder beads and faceted or cut beads, but these are usually best sewn on afterwards as a final embellishment rather than knitted into the fabric itself. Before working with a new bead shape, be sure to carefully check for any sharp edges as these could snag or break the yarn over time.

Sizing

Seed bead sizes are usually given in the format of X/0 – the larger the figure X, the smaller the bead. The most commonly used sizes for knitting are 8/0 and 6/0. Size 8/0 beads work best for more intricate designs where many beads will be used close together and can be used with finer yarn weights from a cobweb to a fine 4-ply; for thicker 4-ply yarns, or when only a few beads are being used, choose a size 6/0 bead. Mixing the two sizes within one stitch pattern can also be very effective so don't be afraid to experiment. Keep in mind that although bead sizes are loosely standardized, they can vary slightly depending on the manufacturer and type of bead. One of the most important aspects of bead selection for knitters is the hole size, as this must be large enough for either a single or doubled length of yarn to pass through (depending on your beading method – *see* Chapter 6). Unfortunately, this information is rarely included in the sizing specifications and does not necessarily relate to the size of the bead itself, so it is often a matter of trial and error. The Japanese brand Toho is a good choice for most seed bead projects, as it is particularly known for large and consistent holes.

Beads come in all shapes, colours and sizes. It's a good idea to keep a supply of silver, gold and black beads to hand as these will work well with most projects.

Colour

Beads are available in a huge range of colours and finishes, from matte to glazed rainbow to crystal. Silver-lined beads are a lovely choice for most projects, as the silver foil within the bead adds extra sparkle – they are available in lots of different colours, but it's particularly useful to keep a supply of clear and gold-coloured silver-lined beads in stock as they work well with any shade of yarn. Metallic-finish silver and gold beads can also be very effective and shiny black beads are great for more subtle embellishments.

Buttons

Buttons can be a source of inspiration in their own right, so it's worth keeping an eye out for any unusual pieces – it is possible to find vintage buttons online or in antique shops, but you may also come across modern buttons with clear Art Deco design influences. A single large statement button or brooch can be used to fasten a loose cardigan or shawl. Alternatively, add small floral buttons to the neck of a sweater for a pretty 1930s feel.

Ribbons and trims

Ribbons and trims can be used in lots of different ways to give your projects a vintage touch. Try sewing a length of ribbon to the wrong side of a button band to add strength and stability to a delicate knitted cardigan or add a length of trim around a cuff or collar. Original ribbons and trims from the 1920s and 30s can be found in antique shops or online and range from white lace trim to intricately patterned ribbons woven from metal and silk. Although they can be expensive, even a small amount can give a unique embellishment to a special project.

Knitting Needles

There are three main types of knitting needles: straight needles, circular needles, and double-pointed needles. Which kind you choose to work with will depend on your personal preferences, so it's worth experimenting with the different types to find your favourites.

Straight needles

The traditional choice, a pair of single-tipped straight needles is often given to beginners. These types of needles are relatively limited as they do not allow you to work in the round and restrict the width of the piece to the number of stitches you can fit on the needle. They are also not the best choice for larger, heavier pieces, as lifting the whole needle as you work

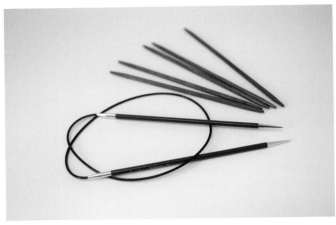

Circulars and double-pointed needles allow you to work small circumferences in the round – experiment with both to find your preferred method.

each stitch can lead to hand and arm strain. That said, many knitters enjoy working with straight needles and there are some very beautiful wooden handmade needles available, so using a pair of 'knitting pins' (as they were often referred to in earlier knitting patterns) can add an authentic vintage feel to your knitting session.

Circular needles

Circular needles are extremely popular and deservedly so. Consisting of two tips connected by a cable, these versatile needles can be used to work projects in the round or flat.

Working flat
Working flat with circular needles is a good choice if you struggle to manipulate straight needles. It's also a much more portable option as you work the stitches using only the short tips, with the majority of your stitches held by the cable. Circular needles are also much better at accommodating high numbers of stitches for shawls and other large projects.

Working in the round

Working in the round can be achieved in multiple ways, depending on your preference. The simplest method is to choose a circular needle that is the same or smaller circumference as your project – circular needles are available in different lengths to accommodate this. You'll begin by casting on enough stitches to cover your circular needle from tip to tip and join to work in the round, then work in rounds with one side (usually this is the RS of the work) facing you the entire time. When using this method, it's important to choose a circular needle length that is smaller than the circumference of the project, as it is very difficult (and potentially damaging to the knitted fabric) to attempt to stretch an insufficient number of stitches around the needle.

If the project circumference is relatively small, such as a sleeve, socks or mitts, a long circular needle (usually 80–100cm/32–40in) can be used with the 'magic loop' method. This technique involves pulling out a loop of cable at the halfway point between stitches, leaving the needle tips free to work the first half of the round before rotating the work and knitting across the second half of the round. Alternatively, two circular needles can be used instead, with each needle holding one half of the round. Tutorials on both of these techniques are widely available online.

Double-pointed needles

Double-pointed needles (or DPNs) are the traditional choice for small circumferences. The stitches are arranged over three or four short DPNs and an additional DPN is used to knit across each section in turn. DPNs are tricky to use on larger circumferences, so you may need to use them in combination with a circular needle depending on the project – many hat patterns, for example, might begin at the brim with a 40cm/16in circular needle, switching to DPNs as the circumference is decreased for the crown.

A note on needle choice

The patterns in this book are generally written to accommodate your preferred needle choice as far as possible. Many of the garments are worked in pieces (allowing the use of straight or circular needles) and the smaller circumference projects are written without reference to specific needle type,

so your preferred method can be used.

Other Tools

Keep these tools to hand when working on the projects in this book.

Tape measure

A tape measure is one of the most important tools in a knitter's collection. Use it to take your own measurements when selecting the correct size to make, to measure the progress of your knitting, or to check your tension. A standard fabric or plastic dressmaking tape measure is fine, although retracting tape measures are extremely convenient to carry with you. Keep in mind that tape measures can stretch out over time and may need replacing.

Ruler

Some knitters find it easier to measure their tension using a rigid ruler rather than a tape measure. You can even find rulers and squares made specially for knitters with 10cm/4in windows cut out.

Scissors

A small pair of embroidery scissors for snipping off ends is very useful for finishing off your knitting and embroidery projects. Keep them sharp by only using them for yarn and thread, never paper.

Tapestry needles

Tapestry needles (or darning or wool needles) are used during the finishing stages of your project, for sewing seams, weaving in ends and grafting live stitches. It's best to choose a blunt-tipped needle for this, to avoid catching and pulling the knitted fabric. Make sure the eye of the needle is wide enough for the yarn to pass through. Keep plenty of tapestry needles to hand – they have a tendency to disappear!

Stitch markers

There are two general types of stitch markers: ring markers and removable stitch markers. Ring markers (often simply referred to as 'stitch markers') are plastic or metal rings that sit on the needle itself, between stitches. They are used in patterns to mark points of shaping or divide sections of a row, but they can also be very helpful to keep track of individual repeats of a complex lace pattern, or to remind you of any changes in stitch pattern. They are particularly useful if you are new to lace knitting, as splitting up each repeat will make it much easier to spot any missed yarnovers or decreases before the end of the row. Feel free to add them to your needles even if a pattern doesn't specify their use – just remember they are less useful for stitch patterns that 'travel' across the row. Removable stitch markers are designed to sit on the knitted fabric rather than the needle. They can be split ring (a ring with an opening) or a locking marker with a clasp. They are useful for marking points on the knitted fabric itself, for dividing up an edge evenly when picking up stitches, or for holding pieces together for seaming. In a pinch, safety pins or small scraps of yarn can also work well as removable stitch markers.

Graph paper and pencils

Graph paper is very useful for creating your own stitch patterns and bead designs, as it allows you to then read your finished design as a chart. However, when using regular graph paper it's important to remember that although one square will represent one stitch when designing, knitted stitches are not perfectly square in practice. This means that your design will look shorter and wider when knit than it appears on regular graph paper, so be sure to test out your design and make any adjustments before using it in your project. Alternatively, you can find special knitting graph paper with correctly proportioned squares online.

Pins

Pins can be a helpful alternative to removable stitch markers. Use them for marking out areas for embroidery, checking your tension or holding pieces together during seaming. Choose longer pins with large heads for easy positioning and removal.

A small, sharp pair of scissors is indispensable and large-headed pins can be very helpful for marking out areas of knitted fabric and seaming.

Understanding Knitted Fabric

Taking the time to develop an in-depth understanding of your knitted fabric is a very helpful step towards a successful project and it can also give you the confidence to explore and experiment with different stitch patterns.

Tension

Tension (also known as gauge) refers to the number of stitches within a specified area of knitted fabric. A good quality pattern should list the required tension, usually giving the number of stitches and rows within a 10cm/4in square. In order to achieve the same finished look and size as your pattern, it is vital to check and adjust your tension to match that given in the pattern. Be wary of terms such as 'standard' or 'average' tension – although each yarn weight does have a general tension range it tends to produce, which can be helpful when comparing yarns, there is no such thing as average or standard when it comes to individual knitters. Tension can vary considerably from knitter to knitter, depending on knitting style and habits. Although you may consider yourself to have an 'average' tension, the designer of your pattern may have a very tight tension, or vice versa.

Achieving the correct tension is a vital step for a successful project. Check your tension by marking out a 10×10cm/4×4" square with pins and counting the number of stitches and rows.

Measuring tension

To measure your tension, work a swatch (a test square) of knitted fabric using the yarn and needles you have chosen for your project. The swatch should be worked over the stitch pattern specified in the pattern if you are following one, or over the stitch pattern that will be used for the majority of the project. This might be simple stocking stitch, or it may be over a more complex stitch pattern. Tension can vary considerably depending on the type of stitch pattern – cables or ribbing, for example, will contract and give a tighter tension than a more open lace – so make sure you are measuring over the correct type of fabric. Your swatch should also be considerably larger than the area to be measured. A 15cm/6in square usually works well and prevents the edge stitches from interfering with an accurate measurement. It can be helpful to work the first and last few stitches and rows of the swatch in a flat stitch pattern such as garter or moss stitch, as these will prevent the edges from curling and make measuring the tension much easier.

After completing your swatch, wash and block it (*see* Chapter 9) in the same way you will your final project. Certain yarns and fibres (such as silk) can grow a significant amount after washing and ignoring this step could lead to a sweater leaving its first wash considerably larger than expected! Many fibres will 'bloom' beautifully with washing, and lace stitch patterns in particular can look completely different after a firm block, so this is the only way to have an accurate idea of your finished fabric. When the swatch is blocked and dry, lay it on a flat surface and measure out a 10cm/4in square in the centre of the fabric – it can be helpful to use pins here to mark out the square. Carefully count the number of stitches horizontally across the measured square. This number is your stitch tension. Next, count the number of rows vertically across the measured square for your row tension. It's a good idea to make a note of these numbers somewhere, along with the yarn and needles that were used.

Adjusting tension

If the measured numbers match those given in the pattern, you can go ahead and get started on your project right away. However, if your tension does not match you will need to adjust your needle size. This is usually straightforward to do. If your tension is too tight (you have more stitches to 10cm/4in than the pattern), you will need to use a larger needle; if your tension is too loose (you have fewer stitches to 10cm/4in than the pattern), you will need to use a smaller needle. Work another swatch and check the tension again before continuing. You may find that you can match your tension stitch-wise but not quite achieve it row-wise. If this is the case, it's best to match the stitch gauge, even if the row gauge does not quite match – it's relatively easy to adjust length by working more or fewer rows. However, it's important to note that if the row gauge is very different it may lead to greater yarn requirements, and you may need to make larger adjustments to the pattern to allow shaped areas to fit correctly.

The value of 'swatching'

Becoming aware of your tension and how to adjust it is very useful when it comes to experimenting with stitch patterns. If you can achieve the same tension over two different stitch patterns, it becomes relatively easy to swap out one for the other when adapting a design. If the two tensions do not match, the difference in numbers between your swatches can allow you to calculate how many stitches you might need to add or remove to achieve the same measurement. Regular 'swatching' will also give you a familiarity with how different stitch patterns behave and the sort of needle size and yarn combinations they work best with – for example, lace stitches often look their best when worked at a relatively loose gauge and in a yarn that relaxes with washing, while cables worked in a plump yarn will 'pop' beautifully in a slightly dense fabric.

Although checking your tension is very useful general practice, and a requirement for producing a successful garment, there are some scenarios in which you can manage without it. A slight variation in the finished size of a shawl, for example, is not necessarily important. Other projects can use such a small number of stitches that a tighter or looser tension is going to produce a minimal difference to the overall size. However, it's a good idea to check that you are happy with the fabric you're producing as you go. Does it drape nicely? How open is the fabric – can you see through it? Is it stiff? Although tension is important, swatching gives you so much more than the numbers – it allows you to get really comfortable with a fabric before investing the hours into a full project, so don't be afraid to unravel and try again if it's not looking quite right.

Reading your knitting

Learning to read your stitches is one of the best ways to gain control and confidence in your knitting. By noting the appearance of each stitch type (knit or purl, increase or decrease), as you work it, you'll begin to learn how your stitches should look, allowing you to spot and fix mistakes much sooner. It's also very helpful for keeping track of your position in a pattern and maintaining a stitch pattern during shaping.

Here are a list of a few common stitches and their appearance – some of which are shown in the Arrow Lace stitch photograph at the end of the chapter. See if you can identify them, then work a swatch (see Chapter 7 for Arrow Lace pattern) to get a feel for the stitches in practice, paying attention to how they appear before, during and after being knit.

Knit stitch – Knit stitches appear as a 'V' shape on one side of the fabric (the side facing you as you work the stitch), and a bump on the other side. One 'V' indicates one stitch widthwise and one row lengthwise. To maintain the appearance of the V on the RS of the fabric, you'll need to knit the stitch on the RS and purl it on the WS.

Purl stitch – Purl stitches appear as a bump on one side of the fabric (the side facing you as you work the stitch), and a 'V' shape on the other side. To maintain the appearance of the

bump on the RS of the fabric, you'll need to purl the stitch on the RS and knit it on the WS.

Yarnover – a yarnover creates a hole in the knitting. On the row immediately following the yarnover row, the yarnover will simply be a strand across your needle – it will feel looser to work into than a regular stitch.

Right-leaning single decreases – A k2tog is identifiable by the right-leaning V it creates – if you look closely at this right-leaning V you'll see it appears to be looped over the top of another, straight V underneath it.

Left-leaning single decreases – As with the right-leaning decrease, you can identify the decrease by looking for a V leaning to left, looped over another V underneath. Left-leaning decreases can look slightly different depending on the method used, but usually only one method is used in a stitch pattern so they're easy to generally identify.

Right- and left-leaning double decreases – Right- or left-leaning decreases can be worked over more than two stitches, in which case the direction of the top-most V will still indicate the type of decrease.

Double decreases – Some double decreases are more centred in appearance. 'Sk2po' will be generally left leaning, as that will be the direction of the top-most V. Beneath this top V there will be a V leaning to the right, then on the bottom of the stack a vertical V. By contrast, a 's2kpo' places the centre V on top so the appearance is much more vertical – almost like a regular knit stitch – with right- and left-leaning Vs stacked underneath it.

The more you practise engaging with your stitches in this way the better you will become at recognizing the appearance and behaviour of certain stitches. Try putting your stitch recognition to the test with the following examples:

- Practise creating diagonal lines with decreases and yarnovers (see Chapter 7), paying attention to the difference between a yarnover and a regular stitch, and noticing how the first stitch of each left-leaning decrease, and second stitch of each right-leaning decrease, stems from the top-most V of the previous decrease.
- When working garment shaping at the waist or sleeve, try reading your knitting to determine when to decrease. If the pattern instructs you to decrease every sixth row,

Arrow Lace uses several different decreases and yarnovers, so it's a good stitch to practise reading your knitting.

you'll need to work straight until you can count five vertical 'V's between the loop on the needle and the right- or left-leaning V of the previous decrease. The next row will create the sixth V, will be the sixth row from the last decrease, and should therefore be a decrease row.

Use your recognition of increases and decreases to help keep stitch patterns correct during shaping – examine how previous stitches such as decreases and yarnovers have aligned to create the pattern up to this point and try to ensure they are falling in the same place as you progress. Keep stitch counts correct by ensuring you are only working a stitch pattern increase if there is also a corresponding decrease, and vice versa.

CHAPTER 6

EMBELLISHMENTS

One of the key elements of style from this period is the use of intricately embellished fabrics. From glittering flapper dresses to delicately pretty 1930s embroidered blouses, simple styles were often lifted with the addition of beaded and embroidered designs at the collar, hem and cuffs. These embellishment techniques can be applied to any garment or accessory, giving a touch of vintage inspiration to the most modern of knitting patterns. Once you've got to grips with the basics, they are also really simple to combine and develop into your own unique designs.

knitwear of the period, the 1920s are well known for beaded evening dresses, and this is a great way to channel some of that glamour into your hand-knit wardrobe.

There are two primary methods of knitting with beads – the method you choose will depend on how precise the bead placement needs to be and your personal preference. For both methods, the hole in the bead will need to be large enough to allow a double thickness of the yarn to pass through it (for more information on bead choice, *see* Chapter 5).

Beading

Beading is a wonderfully easy way to add sparkle to your knitting. Although working more complex beaded designs requires extra attention, the basic beading techniques are easily mastered and even a sprinkling of beads over a design can give an impressive result. Although not extensively used on

The pre-strung method

This method works well if you just want to introduce some sparkle to a plain knitted fabric or very simple stitch pattern. It is more portable than other methods, as all the beads are threaded on the yarn before you begin knitting. However, as the beads are not anchored in place, they can sometimes shift to other stitches, so this method is not recommended when working a beaded lace pattern that requires the beads to stay on specific stitches. It can also become problematic if a large number of beads are placed on the yarn at once, as you will have to push the beads down the yarn as you knit.

Begin by deciding how many beads you will be using at a time. If you run out of beads midway through you will need to cut the yarn, thread more beads on, and rejoin. While this will mean extra ends to weave in, this is often a worthwhile sacrifice as threading large numbers of beads at a time will cause extra friction on the yarn from frequently being pushed along.

There are some other fun options that pre-stringing your

Thread a small needle with both ends of a length of strong sewing thread, to create a loop. Pass the end of your yarn through the loop, so the yarn is folded over the thread.

Remove the sewing needle and thread and begin knitting, pushing the threaded beads down the yarn and out of the way as you work. When you reach a stitch you'd like to bead, bring a bead up the yarn, close to the needle tips.

Place a bead in the needle and draw it down onto the thread, then onto the yarn. Repeat until the desired number of beads are on the yarn.

Work the next stitch, allowing the bead to sit on one of the legs of the stitch.

beads allows you to play with – try adding beaded strands to your knitting.

Work to the point in your knitting that you'd like to place the beaded strand – it should be worked on an RS row. Decide how many stitches you would like your beaded strand to cover. With yarn in front, slip this number of stitches purlwise to the right needle. For this example, I've slipped five stitches.

Bring several beads up the yarn, using enough to cover the length of yarn required to sit across the slipped stitch section. Loosely carry the beaded section along the front of your work so that it sits in front of the slipped stitches, then continue working along your row.

Play around with different lengths to come up with your own designs. Here, fewer stitches have been slipped and fewer beads have been added on each subsequent beading row to create a triangular shape.

The hook method

This method allows you to place beads very precisely on specific stitches so that they remain anchored in place – this is very helpful when working them into complex lace patterns or in stitch patterns where you want the beads to form a clear shape.

For this technique you'll need a crochet hook that is small enough to fit through your chosen bead. A 0.6–0.8mm size hook works well for most projects.

Work to the stitch you would like to bead. You can place a bead on a stitch before or after knitting it – here we will be placing the bead before knitting it. Pick up a bead with the crochet hook.

2

Slip the stitch off the needle and onto the hook. The bead should be sitting on the hook to the right of the stitch.

3

Slide the bead down the hook and onto the stitch. If the bead is quite small you may need to apply a little upward pressure on the hook while easing the bead over with your fingertip.

4

(fourth photo)

Replace the stitch on the needle (again, being careful not to twist it) and knit it.

Designing your own bead pattern

Beading is one of the simplest ways to make your piece unique, as it's so easy to develop your own bead pattern and apply it to an otherwise plain area of knitting. All you need to get started is graph paper and a pencil.

1

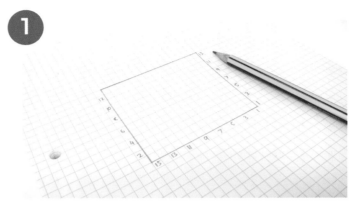

Each square on the graph represents one stitch, so begin by deciding how many stitches and rows you'd like to work your design over – this can be a single motif, or a section that you will repeat across a row. Draw a box around this number of squares – this design will be worked across fifteen stitches and thirteen rows. Number your stitches along the bottom and your rows up the side of the square.

2

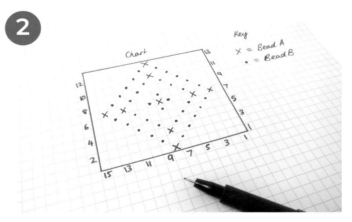

Time to play! Draw a symbol in each square that will have a bead – you can draw a small circle, a cross, or colour it in completely. Use beads in different sizes and colours for a really unique design – draw different symbols to represent each kind of bead and add a key next to your chart. Don't forget you can place beads on both WS and RS rows. Once you're happy with your design, it's a good idea to draw up a clean copy of the chart so that it's extra clear to work from.

Knit your garment or accessory to the point where you'd like to add your bead pattern, then work across your drawn bead chart (either once for a single motif or repeating it as desired). You might find it helpful to place a marker on each side of the charted section to keep track of where it starts and ends. If you are working your piece flat, remember to read RS chart rows from right to left and WS chart rows from left to right; if you are knitting in the round, read all chart rows from right to left.

Thread: You can use regular cotton embroidery thread, or your choice of yarn. The embroidery thread can sometimes sink into the knitted fabric and become less visible, so use a thread or yarn that is slightly thicker than the yarn used for the fabric, or hold it doubled, to get a strong visual effect. For clarity, in the following techniques the word 'thread' has been used to indicate the strand of yarn or thread used for embroidery throughout.

Adding embroidery to your knits is a fun way to play with colour and detail. Experiment with subtle pastels, bright jewel shades or sparkling metallic threads.

Embroidery

Embroidery was hugely popular throughout the 1920s and 30s. As well as being used in the intricately embellished fabrics of 1920s evening wear, it was also included in knitting patterns as a statement feature on an otherwise plain garment. A few basic stitches can turn even the simplest of projects into something exquisitely pretty and absolutely unique. This chapter will cover some of the most popular stitches and how to combine them into motifs, but there are a huge variety of stitches to be explored.

Materials

Needles: You'll need a needle with a large eye, big enough to pass your chosen thread through (if you are going to be using your thread doubled, remember that the eye needs to be large enough to accommodate this also). A sharp-pointed needle is preferable for intricate work, as it will help you work through the knitted stitches as you embroider, but a blunt needle can be used for the simpler outline stitches.

Embroidering your knitwear

Embroidering knitted fabric, particularly hand-knitted fabric, is quite different from working on the standard woven cotton that is more usually associated with embroidery. Here are some tips to keep in mind as you try the following stitches:

- It is important to wash and block your item before embroidering – this will ensure that the knitted stitches are neat and smooth and that the piece is the correct finished size. Otherwise you may find that your stitches – which appeared to lie flat against the knitting before blocking – cause the fabric to pucker as the tension of the surrounding stitches relaxes.

- Whereas you would normally stretch a woven fabric taut before embroidering on it, it is important to handle the knitted fabric lightly and avoid stretching it as you work. Avoid pulling your stitches tightly, and frequently lay the fabric flat to double check that the stitches aren't puckering the surrounding fabric. If you do find there is some slight puckering when you've finished, try blocking the piece again and smoothing the area out – knitting can be very forgiving, and this simple adjustment may fix the problem.

- When inserting the needle and pulling it through, don't be afraid to work into stitches – splitting the yarn – rather than between them. This results in fewer and smaller holes, prevents the knitted stitches from being stretched and anchors your embroidery stitches more firmly in place.

- It can be difficult to unpick embroidery, so draw out the design on paper and make sure you are happy with it before beginning, then use pins or scrap yarn to mark the placement of the design on the section of knitting. If you do make a mistake, use a small pair of sharp embroidery scissors and be very careful not to catch or pull on the knitted fabric as you remove the stitches.

- Be sure to only work with short lengths of embroidery thread at a time – no longer than fingertip to elbow. Pulling a long length of thread through the knitted fabric repeatedly can put a lot of stress on both the thread and the backing stitches, leading to tangles and frayed stitches.

Outline stitches

These stitches work well alone for simple lines, or to outline a shape to be filled in with a filler stitch. They can also be combined to create a wide range of embroidery designs, allowing you to add a unique embellishment to any project. It's a good idea to practise these stitches on a swatch first, carefully controlling the size of the stitches and trying to keep the tension even throughout. When working all of these stitches, secure the thread on the WS of the knitting with a few small stitches before beginning.

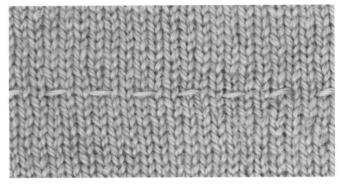

Running stitch.

Running stitch

Running stitch is one of the simplest embroidery stitches, so it's a great place to start when learning to embroider knitted fabrics.

Bring the needle through to the RS at the desired starting point. Insert the needle back into the fabric the desired distance from the starting point, then bring it up again a little further along in a straight line – you can vary how long or short you'd like your running stitches to be, and how much of a gap you'd like to leave. Pull the needle through, then continue in this way, inserting the needle back into the fabric from the RS and out again.

Backstitch

Backstitch is similar to running stitch but creates a continuous line of stitches, without gaps between them. It's very important to avoid pulling on the embroidery thread too hard when working backstitch, as this will cause the fabric to pucker. Instead, gently draw on the thread until it is loosely flush with the knitted fabric.

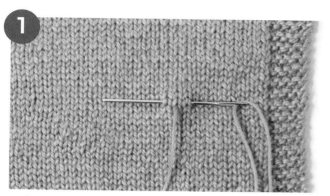

Bring your needle up from the WS one stitch length away from the starting point and draw the thread through. Insert the needle through the starting point, then bring it up again one stitch length ahead of the stitch just made.

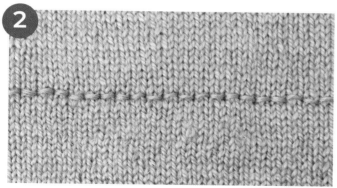

Draw the yarn through, insert the needle through at the end of the last stitch, then bring it up one stitch length ahead. Continue in this way along the desired line. Complete the final stitch by inserting the needle through at the end of the last stitch and fastening off.

Chain stitch

Chain stitch is one of the most versatile stitches – as well as using it for thicker line stitches, it also forms the basis of many floral stitches such as Lazy Daisy stitch. Be very careful not to pull heavily on the thread as you work.

Bring the needle up through the fabric to the RS, then back down to the WS through the same place. Draw the thread through slowly, leaving a small loop of thread on the RS. Bring the needle up to the RS a little further along (how far will depend on how long you'd like each chain stitch to be), bringing it up inside the loop of thread.

Pull gently on the needle until the loop of thread lies flat against the knitting, then insert the needle back into the fabric through the same place it was brought up in the previous step and draw through, leaving a loop on the RS. Bring the needle up through the loop a little further along.

Continue to repeat the last step to create a line of chain stitches. Complete the final stitch by bringing the needle up through the last loop and working a small straight stitch over the loop to anchor it in place.

Heavy chain

This variation on a chain stitch creates a thick, strong line so it's great for more dramatic designs.

Work small stitches close together for a heavy continuous outline, or longer stitches for an open feather look.

Begin by making a single chain stitch anchored by a small straight stitch. The chain stitch should be worked in the opposite direction to the planned stitch line.

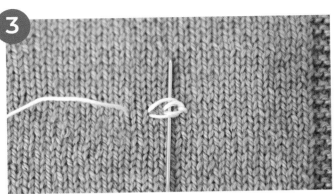

Bring the needle out again a little further along the stitch line from the base of the chain stitch. Insert the needle under the small straight stitch worked in step 1 and draw through.

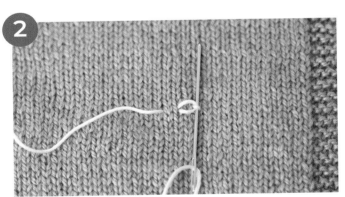

Take the needle back through the fabric at the same point it exited in the previous step, then bring it up a little further along the stitch line. Insert the needle under both of the previous two chains.

Repeat the previous step to create the line of heavy chain stitches. Be sure to always insert the needle under both layers of chain, otherwise it will create a line of regular chain stitches.

Filler stitches

These stitches are used to fill in areas of space, so they're great to use with dramatic, graphic motifs.

Satin stitch

This solid, bold stitch (sometimes known as 'long and short stitch') completely covers an area with long stitches. For this stitch, choose a thicker yarn or embroidery thread held double for a dense finish. If possible, it's a good idea to begin in the middle of the area and work each side of the shape separately. You can also mark the shape out using an outline stitch before beginning if preferred.

Get creative with satin stitch

Satin stitch is versatile. Try showing off the beauty of the knitted background fabric by filling in only part of a shape with satin stitch, leaving the rest plain. This can give your embroidery designs an interesting 'negative space' look. If you are filling a large area, work in layers, blending the sections together by working the stitches up into the previous section. This is particularly effective using different colours to give a shaded effect.

Bring the needle up through the fabric to the RS at the base of the section to be filled, then make a long straight stitch, inserting the needle through at the top of the section. If you have used an outline stitch, your needle should be entering and exiting just outside it.

Repeat the last step to continue filling the space with long straight stitches, varying the stitch length as necessary to adjust to the curves or lines of the shape and working the stitches as close together as possible.

French knot

This is a lovely delicate stitch – add a sprinkling of a few French knots to a design, or work lots of knots close together to fill in a section. It's also a great accent stitch to add to flower motifs.

Bring the needle up through the fabric to the RS at the point where you'd like to work a French knot and draw the thread through. Holding the section of thread closest to the fabric straight, wrap the tip of the needle a couple of times around the strand of thread.

With the wraps still on the needle, insert the needle back through the fabric, very close to the place it exited in the previous step. Keep some tension on the wrapped yarn to keep the wraps in place.

③

Place a fingertip on the little 'knot' on the RS of the fabric and gently draw the thread to the WS until the French knot sits flush to the surface of the fabric, being careful not to pull the knot too tight.

Adding beads

For a really glamorous touch, add beads to your embroidery motifs – try placing one in the centre of flowers, add them to the anchoring straight stitches of the Lazy Daisy or leaf motifs, or add a sprinkling in the background mixed with French knots. To add a bead, bring the threaded needle up to the RS of the fabric, then place the bead onto your length of embroidery thread or yarn – it's helpful if your needle is fine enough to pass through the bead while threaded, but you can also remove the needle, add the bead, then rethread. Anchor the bead in place on the RS with a small straight stitch. If the bead is large, it's a good idea to work another small straight stitch in the same place, passing through the hole of the bead a second time, to secure it.

Floral stitches

Lazy Daisy

Lazy Daisy combines large chain stitches with tiny anchoring straight stitches to create little flowers. It's easy to vary the size and number of petals. You'll work each flower from the centre out.

Bring the needle up through the fabric, then insert the nee-

Lazy Daisy stitch.

dle back into the same place. Draw through, leaving a loop of thread on the RS, then bring the needle back up through the fabric at the desired point of the first petal, ensuring that the needle is running through the loop. Pull on the thread gently, then anchor the loop in place by making a very small straight stitch over the tip of the petal. Repeat this to make the remaining petals, spacing them evenly around the centre point. Add some small chain stitches between the petals in a contrasting colour for leaves or embellish the centre of the flower with a bead.

Leaves motif.

Leaves

You can combine chain stitches with an outline stitch 'stem' for a very effective leaf motif.

Begin by working your stem (or stems) using the outline stitch of your choice – backstitch has been used here. Add leaves along each side of the stem by working chain stitches anchored with a small straight stitch, as in the Lazy Daisy stitch.

Roses

These pretty woven roses are really easy to work but look extra impressive. Although the finished roses have a strong three-dimensional look, most of the embroidery stitches lie on the surface of the knitting rather than repeatedly going through it – this construction means they can be used on very delicate knitted fabrics, as it prevents the distortion that heavy embroidery can sometimes cause to knitted stitches. They are also easy to adjust in size by working longer or shorter straight stitches in step 1. Work large roses using a metallic thread for a dramatic 1920s-inspired look, or smaller roses for a delicate 1930s floral feel.

Draw the thread through gently, miss the next straight stitch, then insert the needle from right to left under the next straight stitch – the thread will lie over the missed straight stitch.

Bring your needle up through the fabric at the centre of the rose, then work five evenly spaced straight stitches out from this centre point. Try to keep them as even and consistent as possible, remembering not to pull tightly on the thread as you complete each stitch.

Continue to repeat the last step around in circles until the straight stitches are completely covered by the woven rounds, then discreetly take the needle to the WS and fasten off.

Bring the needle back through the centre point to the RS. You'll now build up the rose by weaving the thread over and under the straight stitches, working anti-clockwise, so begin by inserting your needle from right to left under one of the straight stitches.

Add a couple of leaves by working a chain stitch anchored by a straight stitch (as in the Lazy Daisy stitch). You can also add a stem using an outline stitch if desired.

Combining the stitches

Once you've mastered the basic techniques above, the creative possibilities are endless and are the perfect way to give any project your own unique touch. Here are some ideas to get you started on your embroidery journey.

Leaf Trellis

This striking design can be repeated continuously as a wide panel, or a few sprigs can be worked for a single motif. For extra sparkle, add beads to enhance the tip of each sprig. This design would look beautiful worked in a metallic thread over a dark colour fabric. It could also be a striking blackwork design if worked in black thread over a pale background. As with any panel motif, it's a good idea to mark the outer edges of the panel area before you begin.

Step 1: Begin at the bottom of the panel, working vertically. Work a length of running stitch diagonally to the right for the stem. Work a chain stitch leaf at the end, anchoring it with a small stitch at the tip. Work two more chain stitches evenly spaced on each side of the top half of the centre stem, leaving the lower half of the stem free.

Step 2: Now work another running stitch stem, beginning halfway down the previous stem, and working diagonally to the left. Add chain stitch leaves around the top half of the step, as before.

Step 3: Continue to work new stems as set, alternating between right and left, starting each stem halfway up the previous stem. Try to keep the running stitch stem parallel with the previous stem below it.

Step 4: Add beads if desired. Using the background yarn (rather than the embroidery thread) when adding the beads gives them a subtle look.

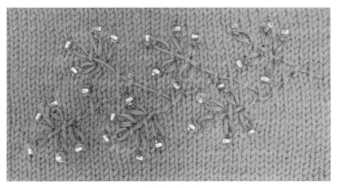

Leaf Trellis.

Rose Trellis

This delicate panel can be worked vertically or horizontally and offers lots of different colour options to play with. Using a metallic thread for the roses and a contrasting bright colour for the vine gives a more dramatic effect. Alternatively, choose a matching green shade for the leaf and vine and work the roses in red, pink or white for a traditional, feminine look. Before beginning, you may find it helpful to use scrap yarn or locking stitch markers to mark the desired outer edges of the panel on your knitting – this will help give you a guideline to follow for the outer points of your vine.

Step 1: Use backstitch to create a curving vine along the centre of your panel area. Try to keep the curves roughly even in shape and size, although some variation adds to the charm of the design.

Step 2: Work woven roses evenly along the vine, alternating sides. Keep the roses of an equal size or vary between large and small according to your preference.

Step 3: Work a leaf opposite each rose by working a chain stitch with a small anchoring stitch at the tip. Place a few more leaves in the spaces between each rose, as desired.

Rose Trellis.

Deco Bursts

This design makes a lovely embellishment for an edge. It looks complex but is actually super simple to work using only a few straight stitches. Here a neutral shade has been combined with a metallic thread for a subtle look, but it can also be stitched in a single shade. Try working it along the button bands of a cardigan or above the ribbing of a sweater. Use the stitches and rows of the background fabric to keep each motif an even size and be careful to only pull the thread until the stitch is flush with the fabric. It's easier to achieve a neat finish if you start each stitch from the outside of the motif and bring the needle in to the central point at the edge.

Deco Bursts.

Crossed Chains.

Step 1: With the first colour, make a long straight stitch perpendicular to the edge of the fabric, then make a short straight stitch parallel to the edge on each side of the base of the centre stitch. Add a medium length straight stitch diagonally on each side, at a 45-degree angle between the two existing stitches. Repeat across the edge, placing the motifs at equal intervals.

Step 2: With the second colour, place two more straight stitches of varying lengths on each side of the central long stitch to create the 'burst' shape. For extra interest, and to anchor down the long centre stitch, work a short horizontal stitch across the central stitch to finish.

Crossed Chains

Embroidery doesn't have to be floral and feminine. This simple combination of chain and straight stitches plays with interlocking lines to create a subtle and distinctive look. These kinds of graphic designs work particularly well with metallic threads and using two shades gives an interesting layered effect. Be sure to use the stitches of the background fabric to keep the stitches neat and evenly spaced throughout.

Step 1: Begin by working a straight line of chain stitches. It is very important to keep each chain stitch the same length, so try to refer to the background knitted stitches as you work each chain.

Step 2: Using the second shade, work long straight stitches to create crosses by bringing the needle out to the RS on one side of the chain line then, working diagonally, passing the needle beneath the chain stitch (between the embroidered stitch and the knitted background fabric) and taking the needle to the WS at an equal distance on the other side of the central line. Repeat in the opposite direction, taking the needle back under

the same chain stitch, to create a cross.

Step 3: Continue to work crosses as described, evenly spacing them along the central chain line.

Deco Leaves

This design uses a traditional motif – a central line of stitches with leaves or flowers worked at opposite intervals – but uses straight stitches to give it a graphic Deco-inspired feel. There are lots of creative possibilities here. For example, try replacing the Deco leaves with regularly spaced 'Deco Bursts', or work the motifs in pairs opposite each other instead of off-set along the chain line.

Step 1: Begin by working a straight line of chain stitches. Backstitch can also be used for this, although the line should be kept strong by working with a thicker yarn or doubled thread.

Step 2: Beginning at the bottom of the chain line, begin adding motifs to each side: work one long straight stitch diagonally out from the chain line, then add four more straight stitches to create a diamond shape around the central stitch. Finally add a horizontal straight stitch connecting the two side points of the diamond.

Step 3: Repeat to add motifs all the way up the chain line, working on alternating sides and spacing motifs evenly every few chain stitches.

Deco Leaves.

CHAPTER 7

CREATING ART DECO FABRICS

Many different stitch patterns can be used to give your fabric an Art Deco feel. This selection offers a starting point but try looking through stitch pattern dictionaries (*see* 'Resources and Further Reading') for more, and don't be afraid to adapt, tweak, combine stitches or add beads to create a unique fabric.

Basic Stitches

Garter stitch

The simplest of the stitch patterns, garter stitch is often the first fabric produced by beginners as it only uses the knit stitch when worked flat (when worked in the round, you'll alternate knit and purl rows). It has the practical benefit of lying flat, without curling, but garter ridges (the row of purl bumps created on the RS when the WS row is knit) are also an easy way to create horizontal lines in your knitting. These horizontal

lines can be incorporated into Art Deco-style fabrics by intersecting them with vertical or diagonal pattern lines. Alternatively, try using them to separate sections of different stitch patterns.

Stocking stitch (or stockinette)

Stocking stitch is simple, smooth, and elegant. It gives a lovely 'blank slate' which you can embellish with panels of more complicated stitches, embroidery, or beading, or it can be left plain for a more pared-down look. Stocking stitch will curl at the edges – to help prevent this, any un-seamed edges are usually finished with a stitch that lies flat, such as rib, garter or moss stitch. When working stocking stitch, the knit side is usually the RS. However, if the purl side is intended to be the RS, it is called reverse stocking stitch. Reverse stocking stitch often 'recedes' when combined with other stitch patterns and causes any knit stitches to appear more pronounced, so it's often combined with cable stitches to make the cable pattern 'pop'.

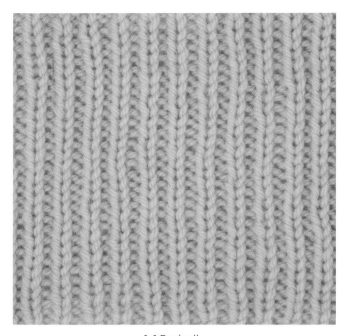

1x1 Basic rib.

Moss stitch.

Worked in the round
Knit every round (or, for reverse stocking stitch, purl every round).
Worked flat
Knit one row, purl one row.

Basic rib (or ribbing)

A basic rib stitch combines knit and purls in the same row or round, to create columns of knit and purl stitches stacked on top of each other. These columns can be wide or narrow, depending on the number of knit/purl stitches used for each column. It's easy to keep track of rib – after you've worked the first row/round (which establishes the knit/purl columns), simply knit the knit stitches and purl the purl stitches as they appear to you. Rib lies flat and is extremely elastic, which makes it very useful for finishing sweaters at the waist, hip, neckline and cuffs. A deep section of rib at the waist is a defining feature of the 1930s sweater, as it stretches enough to fit the high hip while keeping the waist defined. The narrower the columns, the greater the elasticity, which makes 1×1 rib (1 knit column, 1 purl column) the perfect choice for achieving this silhouette.

Worked over a multiple of 2 sts
Worked flat or in the round
Row 1 (RS): [K1, p1] to end.
Rep row 1 for pattern.

For a variation on the 1×1 rib, try working the knit column through the back loop – this adds extra texture, although it is less stretchy than the basic rib.
Worked over a multiple of 2 sts
Worked in the round
Round 1: [K1tbl, p1] to end.
Rep round 1 for pattern.
Worked flat
Row 1 (RS): [K1tbl, p1] to end.
Row 2 (WS): [K1, p1tbl] to end.
Rep rows 1–2 for pattern.

Moss stitch

Like ribbing, moss stitch also mixes knit and purl stitches and results in a flat fabric. However, whereas rib stacks knits upon knits and purls upon purls, moss stitch alternates between the two. It's a good choice for flattening the edges of stocking stitch if you want to avoid creating vertical or horizontal lines,

and don't want the edges to draw in as they will with ribbing.
Worked over a multiple of 2 sts
Worked flat or in the round
Row/Round 1 (RS): [K1, p1] to end.
Row/Round 2: [P1, k1] to end.
Rep rows/rounds 1–2 for pattern.

Linework

The clean look of intersecting and contrasting lines is a key element of Art Deco design. This manifested itself in the fashion of the time in fabric prints and embellishments, as well as in more subtle ways through the use of pleats and tucks in the fabric. The following stitch patterns and techniques are a great way to emulate these details.

Vertical lines

Although ribbing is usually used to shape garments at the waist and cuffs, the strong vertical lines created by rib stitches can also be turned into a decorative feature of the fabric. Rib stitches are easy to customize, making it possible to achieve a huge variety of different patterns – just remember these basic principles:

- Decide how many stitches wide you'd like your columns to be. They can be of equal length, such as columns of 2 knit stitches followed by 2 purl stitches (2×2 rib), or unequal, such as a column of 5 knit stitches followed by 3 purl stitches (5×3 rib).
- Add the stitches from the knit and purl columns together to get your multiple – for example, for a 5×2 rib, you would need a multiple of 7. If you are working in the round, simply cast on the multiple; if you are working flat you might also want to include a final knit column for symmetry – in our example, that would mean you need to cast a multiple of 7 stitches, plus an additional 5 for the final knit column.
- Establish your rib on the first row, then simply knit the knits and purl the purls: an RS knit stitch will appear as a purl stitch on the WS and vice versa. To maintain a rib after the pattern has been established, simply purl or knit the stitch as it presents itself to you.

Vertical lines of ribbing can be used to shape a silhouette or worked as a decorative feature.

3×3 wide rib.

Wide rib

Ribs with wider columns of knit and purl stitches won't pull in as tightly as 1×1 rib – this allows you to block the fabric flat if desired, so that the rib becomes more decorative. They can be combined with intersecting horizontal lines for a clean linework based design or used to give the impression of pleated fabric as in the Margaret cardigan.

Twisted stitches

Try combining a single twisted knit column with a regular wide rib pattern to give a more textured look to some of the vertical lines. Twisted stitches are also great for separating columns of cable or lace patterns.

Beaded columns

Vertical columns of beads are simple to work and can be easily adjusted to give the desired look. Mix them with a regular rib, or simply work them over a plain stocking stitch background.

Horizontal lines

Horizontal lines can be used to separate and highlight different sections of a design, such as decorative areas at the waist,

neck, hip or cuffs. They can also be combined with vertical lines to create clean intersecting patterns that are reminiscent of Art Deco design.

Garter stitch ridges

To create a single garter stitch ridge, work a row of purl stitches on the RS of the fabric (or a row of knit stitches on the WS). You can work a single ridge for a subtle horizontal line, or several rows of garter stitch for a thicker section. Alternatively, space the ridges further apart by working a few rows of stocking stitch between each ridge row.

For an extra special effect, add a row of evenly spaced beads on one of the rows between the ridge rows. This simple technique can be used to add a touch of vintage-inspired sparkle to almost any design and is a lovely way to draw attention to the hip, cuff or waist.

Adding beads between garter stitch ridges creates a sparkling fabric.

Contrast colours

Bands of contrasting colours are an easy way to add horizontal lines to your fabric. For a simple 1920s-sportswear look, work stripes at the hem, cuffs or shoulders.

Knitted fold

This fun technique creates a more pronounced horizontal line

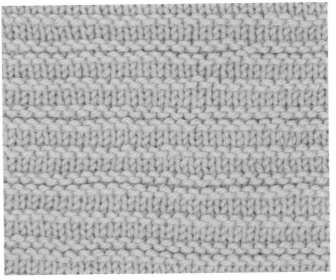

Garter stitch ridges are decorative without being fussy.

Work in stocking stitch for four more rows (you can work more rows here for a larger fold, but it should be an even number). As you knit the next row, you'll work the stitches on the needle together with the stitches picked up from the marked row below.

With RS facing, use the left needle tip to pick up the edge stitch from the marked row directly below the first stitch on the needle. Knit the first stitch together with the picked-up stitch.

Now pick up the purl bump from the marked row directly below the next stitch on the left needle (you might find it easier to use the right needle tip for this) and knit the two stitches together. Continue to repeat this step for each stitch across the row.

and gives the appearance of cords running across the fabric. It can be dropped in to any area of stocking stitch – just remember that it will increase yarn requirements as more rows are worked within the same length. You can work a single knitted fold or several close together for a pin-tucked look. Begin by working to the point in your pattern that you'd like to add the knitted fold, ending with a WS row if working flat, and mark each end of your row with locking stitch markers or pieces of waste yarn.

Diagonal lines

Diagonal lines can be worked alone or combined with vertical and horizontal lines to create more complex Art Deco-style linework designs. Because diagonal stitch patterns 'travel' across the knitted fabric as you work each row, learning to read your knitting (*see* Chapter 5) is especially helpful when working these stitches.

Diagonal 'ribbing'

This technique uses the stacked knit and purl columns of rib stitches but gradually offsets them, so that they travel diagonally across the fabric. On your first row or round, establish your knit and purl columns as with a vertical rib. On every WS row (or even round), maintain the knits and purls as established on the previous row. On every RS row (or odd round), shift the columns one stitch to the right or left: for a right-leaning line, shift the beginning of each column to the right by starting each knit or purl column one stitch sooner; for a left-leaning line, shift the beginning of each column to the left by starting each knit or purl column one stitch later. Diagonal ribbing forms the basis for the Pointed Rib stitch pattern (*see* 'Art Deco Stitch Library: Knit/Purl Stitches').

Decrease lines

Different knitted decreases have their own distinct appearance, and this can be harnessed to create visual lines across the surface of the fabric. Left-leaning decreases include ssk and k2tog tbl, while k2tog will lean to the right. Likewise, double decreases will also have a distinct direction, with sssk and sk2po learning to the left, and k3tog leaning to the right. S2kpo, however, places the centre stitch on top of the decrease and results in a vertical line.

These differences mean that particular decreases can be used to create diagonal lines. For example, to maintain a right-leaning diagonal line across the fabric work regularly spaced k2togs, ensuring that the second stitch of each k2tog aligns with the k2tog on the row below. For a left-leaning diagonal line, the first stitch of each ssk should line up with the ssk on the row below. To keep a stable stitch count and maintain a diagonal line, work an increase after each k2tog, and before each ssk. Keep the line subtle by using an M1 for an invisible increase or work a yo for a pretty diagonal row of eyelets. This sample stitch pattern has 3 sts between each diagonal line, but it can be adjusted for wider or narrower diagonal stripes – always begin by casting on a multiple of (X+2) plus 2, where X is the number of sts desired between each diagonal line.

Row 1 (RS): K1, [k3, k2tog, yo] to last st, k1.
Row 2 and all WS rows: Purl.
Row 3: [K3, k2tog, yo] to last 2 sts, k2.
Row 5: K2, k2tog, yo, [k3, k2tog, yo] to last 3 sts, k3.
Row 7: K1, k2tog, yo, [k3, k2tog, yo] to last 4 sts, k4.
Row 9: K2, [k3, k2tog, yo] to last 5 sts, k5.
Row 10 (WS): Purl.
Rep rows 1–10 for pattern.

Diagonal lines of decreases with eyelet detail.

Cables

Cables are a great way to add diagonal lines to your knitting – they are particularly useful as they allow you to achieve a wide variety of different line thicknesses and angles within the same design. The thickness of the line in cable patterns depends on how many stitches are shifted across the RS of the work – for example, a cable stitch crossing 4 sts over 2 will produce a thicker visual line than crossing 1 st over 2. The angle will depend on how many plain rows are worked between each cable pattern row. Working a cable stitch on every RS row will produce a line with a shallow angle, every fourth row will create a steeper line, and so on. These cable lines can be combined into various stitch patterns, from simple diamonds to intricate filigree-style designs.

Art Deco Stitch Library

Knit/purl stitches

These stitch patterns combine knit, purl and twisted stitches to create subtle but effective fabrics with an Art Deco feel. Many of them draw on the above linework techniques and ideas, mixing vertical knit columns with shifting sections of purl stitches. As with most stitches that combine knits and purls, they have the added benefit of generally lying flat without curling.

Purl Diamonds stitch pattern.

Purl Diamonds

This panel contrasts diamonds of purl stitches with strong columns of knit stitches. The central knit columns are worked through the back loop to make them more pronounced, giving the pattern an impression of depth.

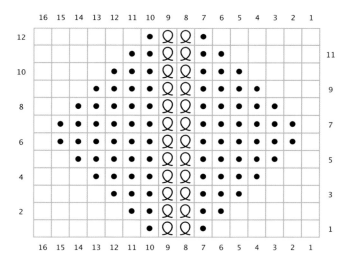

Purl Diamonds chart.

Key

☐	RS: knit WS: purl
●	RS: purl WS: knit
Ω	RS: k1tbl WS: p1tbl

Worked over a multiple of 16 sts and 12 rows

Row 1 (RS): *K6, p1, k2tbl, p1, k6; rep from * to end.
Row 2 (WS): *P5, k2, p2tbl, k2, p5; rep from * to end.
Row 3: *K4, p3, k2tbl, p3, k4; rep from * to end.
Row 4: *P3, k4, p2tbl, k4, p3; rep from * to end.
Row 5: *K2, p5, k2tbl, p5, k2; rep from * to end.
Row 6: *P1, k6, p2tbl, k6, p1; rep from * to end.
Row 7: *K1, p6, k2tbl, p6, k1; rep from * to end.
Row 8: *P2, k5, p2tbl, k5, p2; rep from * to end.
Row 9: *K3, p4, k2tbl, p4, k3; rep from * to end.
Row 10: *P4, k3, p2tbl, k3, p4; rep from * to end.
Row 11: *K5, p2, k2tbl, p2, k5; rep from * to end.
Row 12 (WS): *P6, k1, p2tbl, k1, p6; rep from * to end.
Rep rows 1–12 for pattern.

Pointed Rib stitch pattern.

Pointed Rib

Gradually shifting rib columns are used here to create subtle diagonal lines that appear to grow from a central point. Mark the centre stitch of the row before beginning to make it easier to follow the stitch pattern.

Worked over a multiple of 12 plus 11, and 12 rows

Row 1 (RS): P2, k3, [p3, k3] to centre stitch, p1 for centre stitch, [k3, p3] to last 5 sts, k3, p2.
Row 2 (WS): K2, p3, [k3, p3] to centre stitch, k1 for centre stitch, [p3, k3] to last 5 sts, p3, k2.

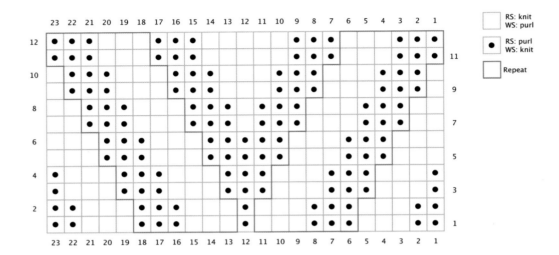

Pointed Rib chart.

Row 3: P1, k3, [p3, k3] to last st, p1.
Row 4: K1, [p3, k3] to last 4 sts, p3, k1.
Row 5: K3, [p3, k3] to centre 5 sts, p5, [k3, p3] to last 3 sts, k3.
Row 6: P3, [k3, p3] to centre 5 sts, k5, [p3, k3] to last 3 sts, p3.
Row 7: Rep row 2.
Row 8: Rep row 1.
Row 9: Rep row 4.
Row 10: Rep row 3.
Row 11: Rep row 6.
Row 12 (WS): Rep row 5.
Rep rows 1–12 for pattern.

Deco Lattice

This subtle stitch pattern blends vertical and diagonal lines by mixing twisted stitches with shifting purl sections to create an interesting all-over lattice.
Worked over a multiple of 14 sts plus 1, and 10 rows
Row 1 (RS): *K1tbl, k4, p2, k1tbl, p2, k4; rep from * to last st, k1tbl.
Row 2 (WS): *P1tbl, p3, k3, p1tbl, k3, p3; rep from * to last st, p1tbl.
Row 3: *K1tbl, k2, p3, k1, k1tbl, k1, p3, k2; rep from * to last st, k1tbl.
Row 4: *P1tbl, p1, k3, p2, p1tbl, p2, k3, p1; rep from * to last st, p1tbl.

Deco Lattice stitch pattern.

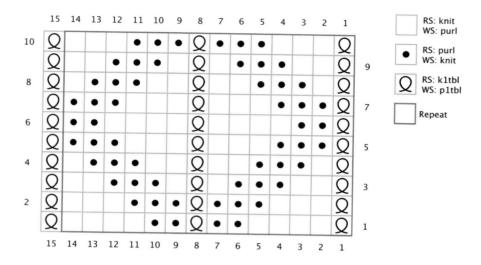

	15	14	13	12	11	10	9	8	7	6	5	4	3	2	1	
10	Q				•	•	•	Q	•	•	•				Q	
	Q			•	•	•		Q		•	•	•			Q	9
8	Q		•	•	•			Q			•	•	•		Q	
	Q	•	•	•				Q				•	•	•	Q	7
6	Q	•	•					Q					•	•	Q	5
	Q	•	•	•				Q				•	•	•	Q	
4	Q	•	•	•				Q			•	•	•		Q	3
	Q		•	•	•			Q		•	•	•			Q	
2	Q			•	•	•	•	Q	•	•	•				Q	1
	Q				•	•	•	Q	•	•					Q	

	RS: knit WS: purl
•	RS: purl WS: knit
Q	RS: k1tbl WS: p1tbl
	Repeat

Deco Lattice chart.

Row 5: *K1tbl, p3, k3, k1tbl, k3, p3; rep from * to last st, k1tbl.

Row 6: *P1tbl, k2, p4, p1tbl, p4, k2; rep from * to last st, p1tbl.

Row 7: Rep row 5.

Row 8: Rep row 4.

Row 9: Rep row 3.

Row 10 (WS): Repeat row 2.

Rep rows 1–10 for pattern.

Ribbed Diamonds

This variation on Purl Diamonds adds extra columns of twisted stitches to the centre of each diamond for a stitch pattern that makes the most of contrasting textures.

Worked over a multiple of 12 stitches plus 1, and 10 rows

Row 1 (RS): *K5, p1, k1tbl, p1, k4; rep from * to last st, k1.

Row 2 (WS): *P4, k2, p1tbl, k2, p3; rep from * to last st, p1.

Row 3: *K3, [p1, k1tbl] 3 times, p1, k2; rep from * to last st, k1.

Row 4: *P2, k2, [p1tbl, k1] twice, p1tbl, k2, p1; rep from * to last st, p1.

Row 5: *K1, p3, [k1tbl, p1] twice, k1tbl, p3; rep from * to last st, k1.

Row 6: Repeat row 4.

Ribbed Diamonds stitch pattern.

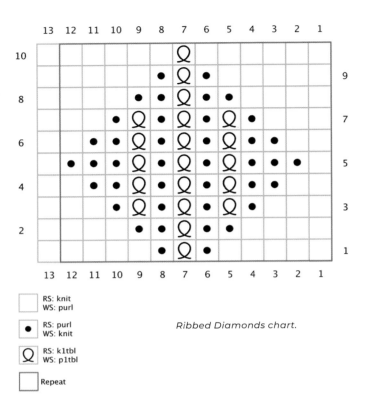

Legend:
- RS: knit / WS: purl (empty square)
- RS: purl / WS: knit (dot)
- RS: k1tbl / WS: p1tbl (Ω symbol)
- Repeat (square)

Ribbed Diamonds chart.

Rib Variation 1 stitch pattern.

Row 7: Repeat row 3.
Row 8: Repeat row 2.
Row 9: Repeat row 1.
Row 10 (WS): *P6, p1tbl, p5; rep from * to last st, p1.
Rep rows 1–10 for pattern.

Rib Variation 1

Getting creative with your rib columns can produce interesting results – here, garter stitch and stocking stitch columns have been mixed with lines of twisted stitches. It's easy to adjust the width of the columns if you prefer a wider rib.
Worked over a multiple of 8 sts plus 2, and 2 rows
Row 1 (RS): *K2, p1, k1tbl, k2, k1tbl, p1; rep from * to last 2 sts, k2.
Row 2 (WS): P2, *k1, p1tbl, k2, p1tbl, k1, p2; rep from * to end.
Rep rows 1–2 for pattern.

Rib Variation 2

This rib pattern shows how adding single columns of twisted

Rib Variation 2 stitch pattern.

stitches between a normal rib can add depth and interest to the lines.

Worked over a multiple of 8 sts plus 3, and 2 rows

Row 1 (RS): *K3, p2, k1tbl, p2; rep from * to last 3 sts, k3.

Row 2 (WS): *P3, k2, p1tbl, k2; rep from * to last 3 sts, p3.
Rep rows 1–2 for pattern.

Zig Zag Rib

This subtle faux-chevron was a popular choice in 1930s sweaters, offering a simple all-over pattern that is clean but eye-catching.

Worked over a multiple of 8 sts plus 1, and 6 rows

Row 1 (RS): [P1, k7] to last st, p1.

Row 2 (WS): K1, [k1, p5, k2] to end.

Row 3: [K1, p2, k3, p2] to last st, k1.

Row 4: P1, *[p1, k2] twice, p2; rep from * to end.

Row 5: [K3, p3, k2] to last st, k1.

Row 6 (WS): P1, [p3, k1, p4] to end.
Rep rows 1–6 for pattern.

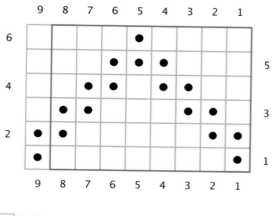

RS: knit
WS: purl

 RS: purl
WS: knit

Repeat

Zig Zag Rib chart.

Zig Zag Rib stitch pattern.

Deco Shells

This stitch pattern combines clever shaping and twisted stitches to create curved shell shapes on a reverse stocking stitch background. For a lacier version of this stitch, replace the M1L and M1R increases with yarnovers. This stitch pattern also looks great on both sides, so it's a perfect choice for projects where the WS will be visible, or you can just pick your favourite side to display as the RS of the fabric.

Worked over a multiple of 15 sts and 16 rows

Row 1 (RS): Knit.

Row 2 (WS): Knit.

Row 3: *P1, M1L, [p1, k1tbl] twice, ssp, k1tbl, p2tog, [k1tbl, p1] twice, M1R, p1; rep from * to end.

Row 4: *K3, [p1tbl, k1] 4 times, p1tbl, k3; rep from * to end.

Row 5: *P2, M1L, p1, k1tbl, p1, ssk, k1tbl, k2tog, p1, k1tbl, p1, M1R, p2; rep from * to end.

Row 6: *K4, p1tbl, k1, p3tbl, k1, p1tbl, k4; rep from * to end.

Row 7: *P3, M1L, p1, k1tbl, k2tog, k1tbl, ssk, k1tbl, p1, M1R, p3; rep from * to end.

Row 8: *K5, p5tbl, k5; rep from * to end.

Row 9: *P4, M1L, p1, ssk, k1tbl, k2tog, p1, M1R, p4; rep from * to end.

Deco Shells stitch pattern.

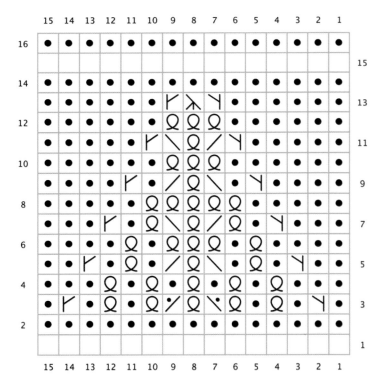

	Symbol	Meaning
		RS: knit / WS: purl
	•	RS: purl / WS: knit
	Q	RS: k1tbl / WS: p1tbl
	/	k2tog
	\	ssk
	✓	p2tog
	✓	ssp
	⅄	sk2po
	Ⳁ	M1R
	⅄	M1L

Deco Shells chart.

Row 10: *K6, p3tbl, k6; rep from * to end.
Row 11: *P5, M1L, k2tog, k1tbl, ssk, M1R, p5; rep from * to end.
Row 12: Repeat row 10.
Row 13: *P6, M1L, sk2po, M1R, p6; rep from * to end.
Rows 14–16: Knit.
Rep rows 1–16 for pattern.

Lace stitches

Lace stitch patterns are created through the careful placement and combination of yarnovers and decreases. Yarnovers create a small hole or eyelet in your work and are made slightly differently depending on whether the stitch following the yarnover is a knit or a purl:

- If the next stitch is to be knit, bring the yarn to the front between the needles (if you have just worked a purl stitch, your yarn will already be in position). As you knit the next stitch, the yarn will cross over the top of the right needle, creating the yarnover.
- If the next stitch is a purl, bring the yarn to the front between the needles, then take it around the right-hand needle tip and back to the front again into position to purl the next stitch. This wrap is the yarnover.

Yarnovers increase a stitch so they are usually paired with a decrease to keep the stitch count even. These decreases will either be right leaning, such as k2tog, or left leaning, such as ssk. Double decreases are also used, such as sk2po, or s2kpo. If you are working shaping at the edges of a lace stitch pattern, keep the stitch pattern correct by keeping track of whether you're able to work an increase/decrease and its corresponding decrease/increase. If you don't have space to work both, you should work neither. Most stitch patterns will resolve their stitch counts across one row (there will be an equal number of increases and decreases) but some can take several rows to return to the correct stable stitch count.

Many lace patterns can have an Art Deco feel to them, especially angular patterns, or those based on leaf or fern shapes. Use them to create fabrics with a luxurious vintage feel, whether it's through a single carefully placed motif (Art Deco Lace), a pretty 1930s-style floral (Floral Lace) or a heavily beaded all-over lace pattern (Feather Lace 1).

Adding beads to lace

Beads have sometimes been added here to give an extra sparkle to the stitches, but they can be left out for a subtler look. Equally, beads can be added to other lace patterns you find. When deciding where to place beads look out for 'spine' stitches, where a knit stitch sits between two yarnovers – these are often the simplest and most effective stitches on which to place beads. Although placing them on yarnovers also works well, avoid placing them on the row immediately following the yarnover row, as this can shrink the eyelet. Throughout this section, beads have been placed using the crochet hook method for an accurate finish (*see* Chapter 6). Knit the stitch after beading it on RS rows and purl the stitch after beading it on WS rows.

Lace Arches

Here s2kpo has been used to create a vertical line of stitches through the middle of each arch – if you'd rather emphasize the curve of the arch, use sk2po as the centre decrease instead.

Lace Arches stitch pattern.

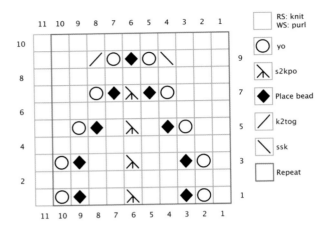

Lace Arches chart.

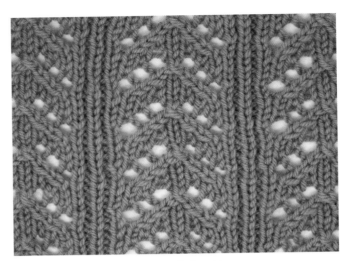

Arrow Lace stitch pattern.

Worked over a multiple of 10 sts plus 1, and 10 rows

Row 1 (RS): *K1, yo, pb, k2, s2kpo, k2, pb, yo; rep from * to last st, k1.

Row 2 and all WS rows: Purl.

Row 3: Rep row 1.

Row 5: *K2, yo, pb, k1, sk2po, k1, pb, yo, k1; rep from * to last st, k1.

Row 7: *K3, yo, pb, sk2po, pb, yo, k2; rep from * to last st, k1.

Row 9: *K3, ssk, yo, pb, yo, k2tog, k2; rep from * to last st, k1.

Row 10 (WS): Purl.

Rep rows 1–10 for pattern.

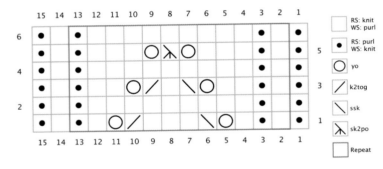

Arrow Lace chart.

Arrow Lace

This simple lace pattern is made up of angular triangles of eye-lets – here it has been combined with a 1×1 rib to enhance the vertical line of the pattern, but see the Josephine sweater for a simpler version of this stitch pattern.

Worked over a multiple of 12 sts plus 3, and 6 rows

Row 1 (RS): *[P1, k1] twice, yo, ssk, k3, k2tog, yo, k1; rep from * to last 3 sts, p1, k1, p1.

Row 2 and all WS rows: K1, p1, k1, *p9, k1, p1, k1; rep from * to end.

Row 3: *P1, k1, p1, k2, yo, ssk, k1, k2tog, yo, k2; rep from * to last 3 sts, p1, k1, p1.

Row 5: *P1, k1, p1, k3, yo, sk2po, yo, k3; rep from * to last 3 sts, p1, k1, p1.

Row 6 (WS): Rep row 2.

Repeat rows 1–6 for pattern.

Trellis Lace

This stitch pattern uses stacked decreases to create offset diag-onal lines. Enhance the lines with beads, or leave the beads out for a more subtle stitch.

Worked over a multiple of 10 sts plus 1, and 8 rows plus 4

Row 1 (RS): *K4, k2tog, yo, pb, k3; rep from * to last st, k1.

Row 2 and all WS rows: Purl.

Row 3: *K3, k2tog, yo, pb, k4; rep from * to last st, k1.

Row 5: *K2, k2tog, yo, pb, yo, ssk, k3; rep from * to last st, k1.

Row 7: *K1, k2tog, yo, pb, k1, pb, yo, ssk, k2; rep from * to last st, k1.

Trellis Lace stitch pattern.

Row 9: *K4, k2tog, yo, pb, yo, ssk, k2.
Row 11: *K3, k2tog, yo, pb, k1, pb, yo, ssk; rep from * to last st, k1.
Row 12 (WS): Purl.
Rep rows 5–12 for pattern.

Art Deco Lace

The straight lines of iconic Art Deco diamond designs are perfect for translating into lace with directional decreases. This motif can be used alone or repeated across larger projects such as shawls and scarves.
Worked over a multiple of 13 sts plus 2, and 22 rows
Row 1 (RS): K1, *k4, k2tog, yo, pb, yo, ssk, k4; rep from * to last st, k1.

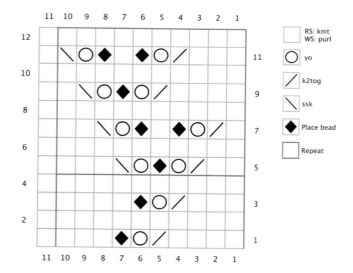

Trellis Lace chart.

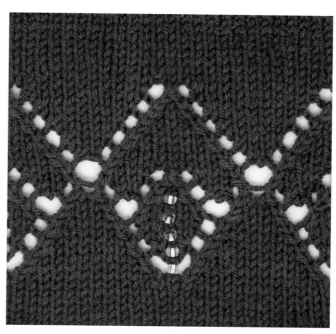

Art Deco Lace motif.

Rows 2, 4 & 6 (WS): Purl.
Row 3: K1, *k3, k2tog, yo, k1, pb, k1, yo, ssk, k3; rep from * to last st, k1.
Row 5: K1, *k2, k2tog, yo, k2, pb, k2, yo, ssk, k2; rep from * to last st, k1.
Row 7: K1, *k1, k2tog, yo twice, ssk, k1, pb, k1, k2tog, yo twice, ssk, k1; rep from * to last st, k1.

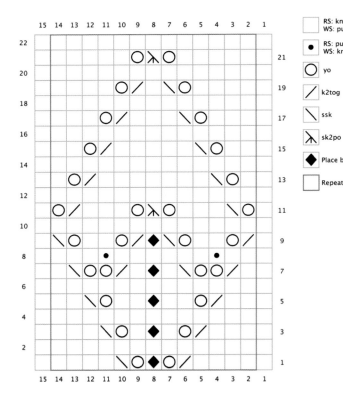

Art Deco Lace chart.

Chandelier Lace 1

This stitch pattern uses twisted 1×1 rib alongside clever shaping to create curved motifs. Adding beads accents the shaping and gives the fabric weight but can be left out if preferred. This pattern results in a gently scalloped edge, so working rows 1–12 once at the beginning of the project creates a lovely edging or hem.

Worked over a multiple of 14 sts plus 1, and 12 rows

Row 1 (RS): *Pb, yo, [k1tbl, p1] twice, k1tbl, sk2po, [k1tbl, p1] twice, k1tbl, yo; rep from * to last st, pb.

Row 2 (WS): P1, *[p1, p1tbl, k1, p1tbl, k1, p1tbl] twice, p2; rep from * to end.

Row 3: *K1, pb, yo, [k1tbl, p1] twice, sk2po, [p1, k1tbl] twice, yo, pb; rep from * to last st, k1.

Row 4: P1, *p2, [p1tbl, k1] twice, p1, [k1, p1tbl] twice, p3; rep from * to end.

Row 5: *K2, pb, yo, k1tbl, p1, k1tbl, sk2po, k1tbl, p1, k1tbl, yo, pb, k1; rep from * to last st, k1.

Row 6: P1, *p3, p1tbl, k1, p1tbl, p1, p1tbl, k1, p1tbl, p4; rep from * to end.

Row 7: *K3, pb, yo, k1tbl, p1, sk2po, p1, k1tbl, yo, pb, k2; rep from * to last st, k1.

Row 8: P1, *p4, p1tbl, k1, p1, k1, p1tbl, p5; rep from * to end.

Row 9: *K4, pb, yo, k1tbl, sk2po, k1tbl, yo, pb, k3; rep from

Row 8: Purl, working (p1, k1) in each double yo.
Row 9: K1, *k2tog, yo, k2, yo, ssk, pb, k2tog, yo, k2, yo, ssk; rep from * to last st, k1.
Row 10: Purl.
Row 11: K1, *yo, ssk, k3, yo, sk2po, yo, k3, k2tog, yo; rep from * to last st, k1.
Row 12: Purl, working (p1, k1) in each double yo.
Row 13: K1, *k1, yo, ssk, k7, k2tog, yo, k1; rep from * to last st, k1.
Rows 14, 16, 18, 20 and 22: Rep row 10.
Row 15: K1, *k2, yo, ssk, k5, k2tog, yo, k2; rep from * to last st, k1.
Row 17: K1, *k3, yo, ssk, k3, k2tog, yo, k3; rep from * to last st, k1.
Row 19: K1, *k4, yo, ssk, k1, k2tog, yo, k4; rep from * to last st, k1.
Row 21: K1, *k5, yo, sk2po, yo, k5; rep from * to last st, k1.
Rep rows 1–22 for pattern.

Chandelier Lace 1 stitch pattern.

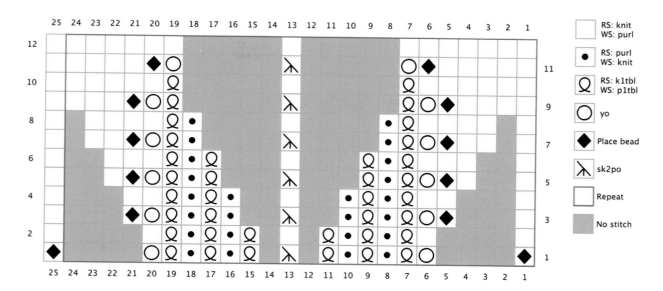

Chandelier Lace 1 chart.

* to last st, k1.

Row 10: P1, *p5, p1tbl, p1, p1tbl, p6; rep from * to end.

Row 11: *K5, pb, yo, sk2po, yo, pb, k4; rep from * to last st, k1.

Row 12 (WS): Purl.

Rep rows 1–12 for pattern.

Chandelier Lace 2

This more complex version of Chandelier Lace requires some concentration but produces a beautifully intricate fabric that is well worth the effort, with or without beads.

Worked over a multiple of 14 sts plus 8, and 24 rows

Row 1 (RS): K2tog, [k1tbl, p1] twice, k1tbl, yo, *pb, yo, [k1tbl, p1] twice, k1tbl, sk2po, [k1tbl, p1] twice, k1tbl, yo; rep from * to last st, pb.

Row 2 (WS): P1tbl, *[p1, p1tbl, k1, p1tbl, k1, p1tbl] twice, p1, p1tbl; rep from * to last 7 sts, p1, [p1tbl, k1] twice, p1tbl, p1.

Row 3: K2tog, [p1, k1tbl] twice, yo, pb, *k1tbl, pb, yo, [k1tbl, p1] twice, sk2po, [p1, k1tbl] twice, yo, pb; rep from * to last st, k1tbl.

Row 4: P1tbl, *k1, p1, [p1tbl, k1] twice, p1, [k1, p1tbl] twice, p1, k1, p1tbl; rep from * to last 7 sts, k1, p1, [p1tbl, k1] twice, p1.

Chandelier Lace 2 stitch pattern.

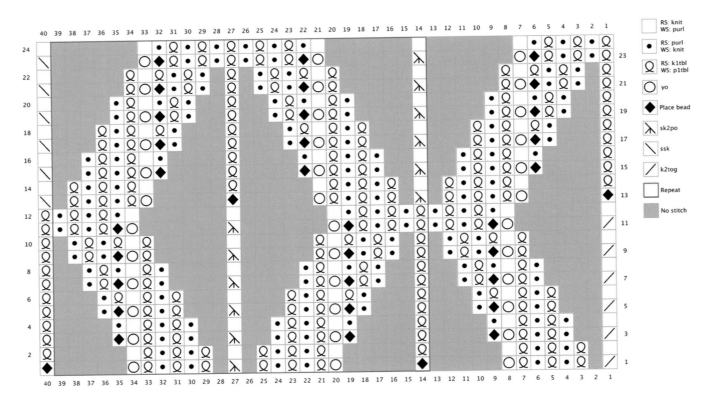

Chandelier Lace 2 chart.

Row 5: K2tog, k1tbl, p1, k1tbl, yo, pb, p1, *k1tbl, p1, pb, yo, k1tbl, p1, k1tbl, sk2po, k1tbl, p1, k1tbl, yo, pb, p1; rep from * to last st, k1tbl.

Row 6: P1tbl, *[k1, p1tbl, p1, p1tbl] 3 times, k1, p1tbl; rep from * to last 7 sts, k1, p1tbl, p1, p1tbl, k1, p1tbl, p1.

Row 7: K2tog, p1, k1tbl, yo, pb, k1tbl, p1, *k1tbl, p1, k1tbl, pb, yo, k1tbl, p1, sk2po, p1, k1tbl, yo, pb, k1tbl, p1; rep from * to last st, k1tbl.

Row 8: P1tbl, *k1, [p1tbl, k1, p1] twice, k1, p1tbl, p1, [k1, p1tbl] twice; rep from * to last 7 sts, k1, [p1tbl, k1, p1] twice.

Row 9: K2tog, k1tbl, yo, pb, p1, k1tbl, p1, *[k1tbl, p1] twice, pb, yo, k1tbl, sk2po, k1tbl, yo, pb, p1, k1tbl, p1; rep from * to last st, k1tbl.

Row 10: P1tbl, *k1, p1tbl, k1, [p1tbl, p1] 3 times, [p1tbl, k1] twice, p1tbl; rep from * to last 7 sts, [k1, p1tbl] twice, p1, p1tbl, p1.

Row 11: K2tog, yo, pb, [k1tbl, p1] twice, *[k1tbl, p1] twice, k1tbl, pb, yo, sk2po, yo, pb, [k1tbl, p1] twice; rep from * to last st, k1tbl.

Row 12: P1tbl, *[k1, p1tbl] twice, k1, p3, k1, [p1tbl, k1] twice, p1tbl; rep from * to last 7 sts, k1, p1tbl, p1, p1tbl, k1, p1tbl, p1.

Row 13: Pb, yo, [k1tbl, p1] twice, k1tbl, *sk2po, [k1tbl, p1] twice, k1tbl, yo, pb, yo, [k1tbl, p1] twice, k1tbl; rep from * to last 2 sts, ssk.

Row 14: P1, *[p1tbl, k1] twice, [p1tbl, p1] twice, [p1tbl, k1] twice, p1tbl, p1; rep from * to last 7 sts, [p1tbl, k1] twice, p1tbl, p1, p1tbl.

Row 15: K1tbl, pb, yo, [k1tbl, p1] twice, *sk2po, [p1, k1tbl] twice, yo, pb, k1tbl, pb, yo, [k1tbl, p1] twice; rep from * to last 2 sts, ssk.

Row 16: P1, *[k1, p1tbl] twice, p1, k1, p1tbl, k1, p1, [p1tbl, k1] twice, p1; rep from * to last 7 sts, [k1, p1tb] twice, p1, k1, p1tbl.

Row 17: K1tbl, p1, pb, yo, k1tbl, p1, k1tbl, *sk2po, k1tbl, p1, k1tbl, yo, pb, p1, k1tbl, p1, pb, yo, k1tbl, p1, k1tbl; rep from * to last 2 sts, ssk.

Row 18: P1, *p1tbl, k1, p1tbl, p1, [p1tbl, k1] twice, p1tbl, p1,

Feather Lace 1 stitch pattern.

or leaf-like effect, omit the beads.

Worked over a multiple of 14 sts plus 2, and 12 rows

Row 1 (RS): K1, *k8, yo, pb, yo, k2, sssk; rep from * to last st, k1.

Row 2 and all WS rows: Purl.

Row 3: K1, *k6, pb, k2, yo, pb, yo, k1, sssk; rep from * to last st, k1.

Row 5: K1, *k3tog, k3, yo, pb, yo, k3, yo, pb, yo, sssk; rep from * to last st, k1.

Row 7: K1, *k3tog, k2, yo, pb, yo, k8; rep from * to last st, k1.

Row 9: K1, *k3tog, k1, yo, pb, yo, k2, pb, k6; rep from * to last st, k1.

Row 11: K1, *k3tog, yo, pb, yo, k3, yo, pb, yo, k3, sssk; rep from * to last st, k1.

Row 12 (WS): Purl.

Rep rows 1–12 for pattern.

p1tbl, k1, p1tbl, p1; rep from * to last 7 sts, p1tbl, k1, p1tbl, p1, p1tbl, k1, p1tbl.

Row 19: K1tbl, p1, k1tbl, pb, yo, k1tbl, p1, *sk2po, p1, k1tbl, yo, pb, [k1tbl, p1] twice, k1tbl, pb, yo, k1tbl, p1; rep from * to last 2 sts, ssk.

Row 20: P1, *k1, p1tbl, p1, [k1, p1tbl] twice, k1, [p1tbl, k1] twice; rep from * to last 7 sts k1, p1tbl, p1, [k1, p1tbl] twice.

Row 21: [K1tbl, p1] twice, pb, yo, k1tbl, *sk2po, k1tbl, yo, pb, [p1, k1tbl] 3 times, p1, pb, yo, k1tbl; rep from * to last 2 sts, ssk.

Row 22: P1, *p1tbl, p1, [p1tbl, k1] 4 times, p1tbl, p1, p1tbl, p1; rep from * to last 7 sts, p1tbl, p1, [p1tbl, k1] twice, p1tbl.

Row 23: [K1tbl, p1] twice, k1tbl, pb, yo, *sk2po, yo, pb, [k1tbl, p1] 4 times, k1tbl, pb, yo; rep from * to last 2 sts, ssk.

Row 24 (WS): P1, *p1, k1, [p1tbl, k1] 5 times, p2; rep from * to last 7 sts, p1, k1, [p1tbl, k1] twice, p1tbl.

Rep rows 1–24 for pattern.

Feather Lace 1

The feather shaped motifs of this stitch pattern are enhanced with the addition of beads along the 'spine' – for a more fern

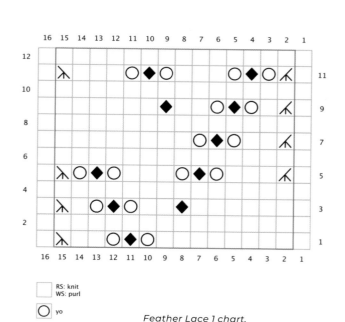

Feather Lace 1 chart.

☐	RS: knit / WS: purl
Ⓞ	yo
人	sssk
木	k3tog
◆	Place bead
☐	Repeat

Feather Lace 2

The beads in this stitch pattern are carefully placed to create the curved feather shapes – omitting them will give you a minimalist pattern of regularly spaced diagonal lines instead.

Worked over a multiple of 13 sts and 16 rows plus 2

Row 1 (RS): [K7, yo, ssk, k4] to end.

Rows 2, 4 & 6 (WS): Purl.

Row 3: [K7, pb, yo, ssk, k3] to end.

Row 5: [K7, pb, k1, yo, ssk, k2] to end.

Row 7: [K8, pb, k1, yo, ssk, k1] to end.

Row 8: [P3, pb, p9] to end.

Row 9: [K4, k2tog, yo, k4, pb, k2] to end.

Row 10: [Pb, p12] to end.

Row 11: [K3, k2tog, yo, pb, k7] to end.

Rows 12 & 14: Purl.

Row 13: [K2, k2tog, yo, k1, pb, k7] to end.

Row 15: [K1, k2tog, yo, k1, pb, k8] to end.

Row 16: [P9, pb, p3] to end.

Row 17: [K2, pb, k4, yo, ssk, k4] to end.

Row 18 (WS): [P12, pb] to end.

Rep rows 3–18 for pattern.

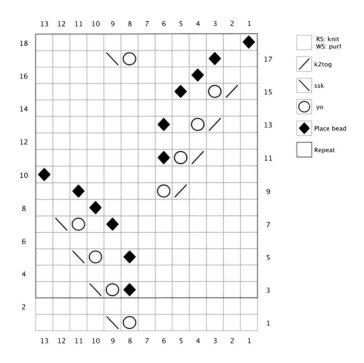

Feather Lace 2 chart.

Feather Lace 2 stitch pattern.

Leaf Lace

This traditional leaf-shaped lace pattern is given a bit of extra depth and texture with the addition of a purl edging around the motifs.

Worked over a multiple of 14 sts plus 17, and 16 rows

Row 1 (RS): K4, k2tog, p2, yo, pb, yo, *p2, ssk, k5, k2tog, p2, yo, pb, yo; rep from * to last 8 sts, p2, ssk, k4.

Row 2 and all WS rows: Purl.

Row 3: K3, k2tog, p2, k1, yo, pb, yo, k1, *p2, ssk, k3, k2tog, p2, k1, yo, pb, yo, k1; rep from * to last 7 sts, p2, ssk, k3.

Row 5: K2, k2tog, p2, k2, yo, pb, yo, k2, *p2, ssk, k1, k2tog, p2, k2, yo, pb, yo, k2; rep from * to last 6 sts, p2, ssk, k2.

Row 7: K1, k2tog, p2, k3, yo, pb, yo, k3, *p2, sk2po, p2, k3, yo, pb, yo, k3; rep from * to last 5 sts, p2, ssk, k1.

Row 9: K1, pb, yo, p2, ssk, k5, k2tog, *p2, yo, pb, yo, p2, ssk, k5, k2tog; rep from * to last 4 sts, p2, yo, pb, k1.

Row 11: K1, pb, yo, k1, p2, ssk, k3, k2tog, *p2, k1, yo, pb, yo, k1, p2, ssk, k3, k2tog; rep from * to last 5 sts, p2, k1, yo, pb, k1.

Leaf Lace stitch pattern.

Row 13: K1, pb, yo, k2, p2, ssk, k1, k2tog, *p2, k2, yo, pb, yo, k2, p2, ssk, k1, k2tog; rep from * to last 6 sts, p2, k2, yo, pb, k1.

Row 15: K1, pb, yo, k3, p2, sk2po, *p2, k3, yo, pb, yo, k3, p2, sk2po; rep from * to last 7 sts, p2, k3, yo, pb, k1.

Row 16 (WS): Purl.

Rep rows 1–16 for pattern.

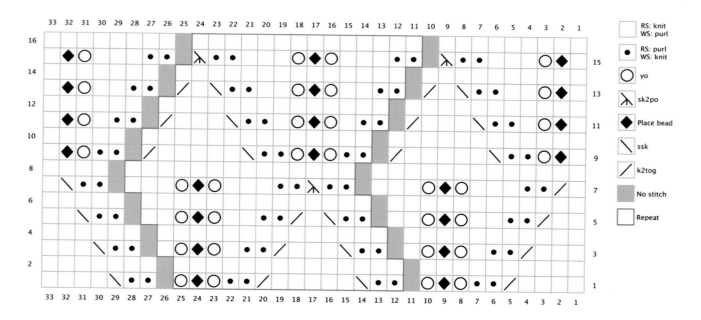

Leaf Lace chart.

Floral Lace

Many blouses and dresses from the 1930s were sewn from delicate floral prints – this simple lace pattern is an homage to these pretty chintz designs and offers plenty of scope for playing with bead and yarn colour combinations. If you prefer it without beads, omit them and try adding a bobble to the spine stitch between the yarnovers on rows 5 and 11 as follows: work to the spine stitch, (k1, yo, k1) into the spine stitch, turn work, p3, turn work, sk2po, continue with the pattern as indicated. The sample photograph shows a mix of the two methods.

Worked over a multiple of 10 sts plus 2, and 12 rows

Row 1 (RS): Knit.

Row 2 (WS): Purl.

Row 3: K1, *k5, k2tog, yo, k1, yo, ssk; rep from * to last st, k1.

Row 4: P1, *p2, pb, p7; rep from * to last st, p1.

Row 5: K1, *k6, [pb, k1] twice; rep from * to last st, k1.

Row 6: Rep row 4.

Row 7: Knit.

Row 8: Purl.

Row 9: K1, *k2tog, yo, k1, yo, ssk, k5; rep from * to last st, k1.

Row 10: P1, *p7, pb, p2; rep from * to last st, p1.

Row 11: K1, *[k1, pb] twice, k6; rep from * to last st, k1.

Row 12 (WS): Rep row 10.

Rep rows 1–12 for pattern.

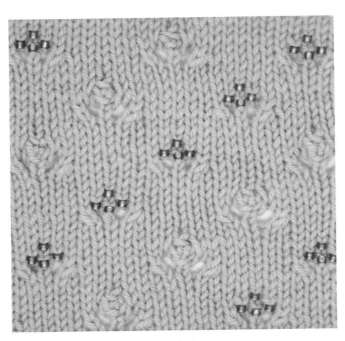

Floral Lace stitch pattern.

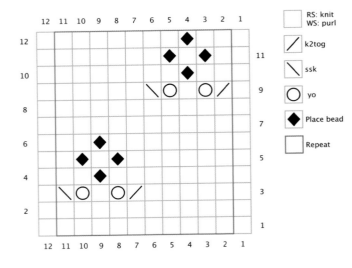

Floral Lace chart.

Lace Rib

For an alternative to a plain rib stitch, try replacing some of the columns with a simple lace stitch panel. Here, beads have also been added to the alternate knit columns for a glamorous look. Remember that decorative ribs like this will not pull in as much as a regular rib, so use this stitch for edges that need to be flat but not elastic.

Worked over a multiple of 12 sts plus 9, and 4 rows

Row 1 (RS): K3, [p3, k3] to end.
Row 2 (WS): P3, [k3, p3] to end.
Row 3: K3, [p3, yo, sk2po, yo, p3, k3] to last 6 sts, p3, k3.
Row 4 (WS): Rep row 2.
Rep rows 1–4 for pattern.

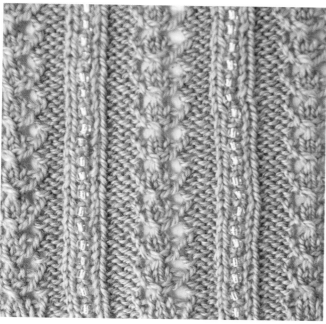

Lace Rib stitch pattern.

Cable stitches

Cables are created by rearranging stitches and working them in a new order, so that one or more stitches cross to the right or left on the front of the work. This can involve simply knitting the stitches in the new order, or mixing knits, purls and twisted stitches within the same cable, depending on the desired effect. There are many different ways to abbreviate cables – this book uses the X/Y system, where X number of stitches are crossed over Y number of stitches. R or L indicates whether the cable leans to the right or left, while 'P' and 'T' suggests whether purl or twisted stitches are involved. The stitches travelling across the RS of the fabric will nearly always

Jewelled Lattice stitch pattern.

Adding beads to cables

Beads can be added to cables to highlight particular focal points. Try adding them to the centre of small cable crosses (as in Cable Rib 2), sprinkling them through the centre of larger motifs (as in Beaded Diamond Panel) or even use them to trace the outer edge of the cables in a panel, placing them one or two stitches before the first cable and after the last cable. Throughout this section, beads have been placed using the crochet hook method for an accurate finish (see Chapter 6). Knit the stitch after beading it on RS rows and purl the stitch after beading it on WS rows.

be knit. Thus a 3/2 RPC is a cable where three knit stitches are crossed to the right over two purl stitches. As with a rib stitch pattern, the knits and purls are usually maintained in pattern as you work the wrong side, so that a column of knit stitches is shifted across a reverse stocking stitch or rib background. The interplay between diagonal and vertical lines that can be created with cables make them perfect for replicating Art Deco motifs and patterns. This is a very small selection of possible cable stitch patterns, but whole stitch dictionaries of cable patterns are available and can be a rich source of inspiration for creating Art Deco-style fabrics.

Jewelled Lattice

This vertical panel combines rope cables at each side with a central lattice worked over a reverse stocking stitch back-

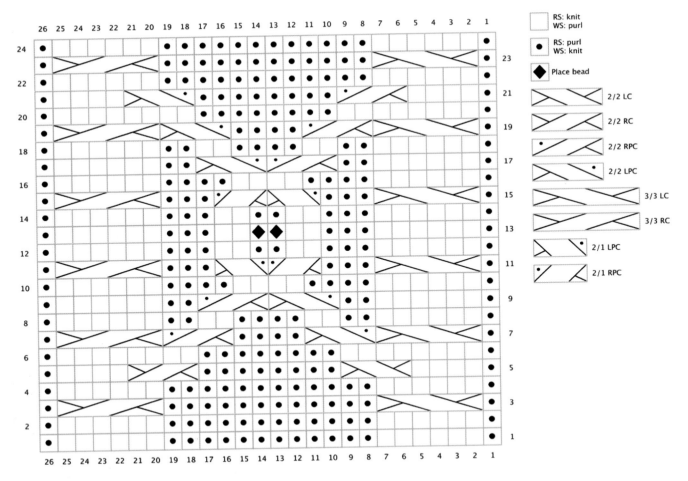

Jewelled Lattice chart.

ground. Beads are placed in the centre of each meeting point between the diagonal cable lines to give a subtle sparkle to the design.

Worked over 26 sts and 24 rows

Row 1 (RS): P1, k6, p12, k6, p1.
Row 2 (WS): K1, p6, k12, p6, k1.
Row 3: P1, 3/3 LC, p12, 3/3 RC, p1.
Row 4: Rep row 2.
Row 5: P1, k4, 2/2 LC, p8, 2/2 RC, k4, p1.
Row 6: K1, p8, k8, p8, k1.
Row 7: P1, 3/3 LC, 2/2 LPC, p4, 2/2 RPC, 3/3 RC, p1.
Row 8: K1, p6, k2, p2, k4, p2, k2, p6, k1.
Row 9: P1, k6, p2, 2/2 LPC, 2/2 RPC, p2, k6, p1.
Row 10: K1, p6, k4, p4, k4, p6, k1.
Row 11: P1, 3/3 LC, p3, 2/1 RPC, 2/1 LPC, p3, 3/3 RC, p1.
Row 12: K1, p6, k3, p2, k2, p2, k3, p6, k1.
Row 13: P1, k6, p3, k2, pb twice, k2, p3, k6, p1.
Row 14: Rep row 12.
Row 15: P1, 3/3 LC, p3, 2/1 LPC, 2/1 RPC, p3, 3/3 RC, p1.
Row 16: Rep row 10.
Row 17: P1, k6, p2, 2/2 RPC, 2/2 LPC, p2, k6, p1.
Row 18: Rep row 8.
Row 19: P1, 3/3 LC, 2/2 RPC, p4, 2/2 LPC, 3/3 RC, p1.
Row 20: Rep row 6.
Row 21: P1, k4, 2/2 RPC, p8, 2/2 LPC, k4, p1.
Row 22: Rep row 2.
Row 23: Rep row 1.
Row 24: Rep row 2.
Rep rows 1–24 for pattern.

Cabled Rib 1

Adding simple rope cables to your ribbing is a lovely way to enhance the hem and cuffs of a garment. You can place the cables at regular intervals, or – as here – vary the number of rows worked in between each cable for different effects. The size of cable you use will depend on the size of the knit column – here a 2/2 cable is worked over a 4-st column, but you could work a 3/3 cable over a 6-st column, a 2/3 cable over a 5-st column, and so on.

Worked over a multiple of 10 sts plus 6, and 18 rows plus 4

Row 1 (RS): *P2, k2, p2, k4; rep from * to last 6 sts, p2, k2, p2.
Row 2 and all WS rows: K2, p2, k2, *p4, k2, p2, k2; rep from * to end.
Row 3: *P2, k2, p2, 2/2 LC; rep from * to last 6 sts, p2, k2, p2.
Row 5: Rep row 3.
Row 7: Rep row 1.
Row 9: Rep row 3.
Row 11: Rep row 1.
Row 13: Rep row 1.
Row 15: Rep row 3.
Row 17: Rep row 1.
Row 19: Rep row 3.
Row 20 (WS): Rep row 2.

Cabled Rib 1 stitch pattern.

Rep rows 3–20 for pattern, then complete the rib as follows:
Row 21 (RS): Rep row 3.
Row 22 (WS): Rep row 2.

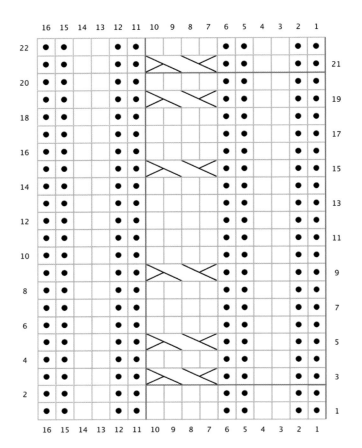

Cabled Rib 2 stitch pattern.

Cabled Rib 1 chart.

☐	RS: knit WS: purl
●	RS: purl WS: knit
✕	2/2 LC
☐	Repeat

Cabled Rib 2

This slightly more complex cabled rib variation uses larger cables enhanced with a bead at the centre of each twist for a glamorous look.

Worked over a multiple of 14 sts plus 3, and 14 rows

Row 1 (RS): *K3, p3, k2, p1, k2, p3; rep from * to last 3 sts, k3.

Row 2 (WS): P3, *k3, p2, k1, p2, k3, p3; rep from * to end.

Rows 3–4: Rep rows 1–2.

Row 5: *K3, p3, 2/1/2 RPC, p3; rep from * to last 3 sts, k3.

Row 6: Rep row 2.

Row 7: *K3, p2, 2/1 RPC, p1, 2/1 LPC, p2; rep from * to last 3 sts, k3.

Row 8: P3, *k2, p2, k1, pb, k1, p2, k2, p3; rep from * to end.

Row 9: *K3, p2, 2/1 LPC, p1, 2/1 RPC, p2; rep from * to last 3 sts, k3.

Row 10: Rep row 2.

Row 11: Rep row 5.

Row 12: Rep row 2.

Row 13: Rep row 1.

Row 14 (WS): Rep row 2.

Rep rows 1–14 for pattern.

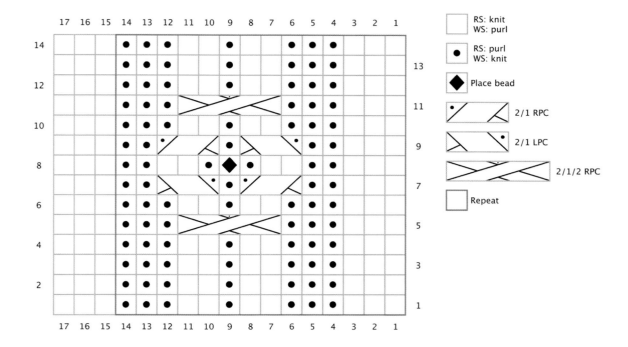

	17	16	15	14	13	12	11	10	9	8	7	6	5	4	3	2	1	
14				●	●	●			●			●	●	●				
				●	●	●			●			●	●	●				13
12				●	●	●			●			●	●	●				
				●	●	●			●			●	●	●				11
10				●	●	●						●	●	●				
				●	●	●			●			●	●	●				9
8				●	●	●		●	◆	●		●	●	●				
				●	●	●						●	●	●				7
6				●	●	●			●			●	●	●				
				●	●	●			●			●	●	●				5
4				●	●	●			●			●	●	●				
				●	●	●			●			●	●	●				3
2				●	●	●			●			●	●	●				
				●	●	●			●			●	●	●				1
	17	16	15	14	13	12	11	10	9	8	7	6	5	4	3	2	1	

Legend:
- □ RS: knit / WS: purl
- ● RS: purl / WS: knit
- ◆ Place bead
- 2/1 RPC
- 2/1 LPC
- 2/1/2 RPC
- □ Repeat

Cabled Rib 2 chart.

1x1 Diamond Cables stitch pattern.

1×1 Diamond Cables

These subtle cabled diamonds sit on a background of 1×1 rib, allowing the diagonal lines of the cable to contrast with the vertical lines of rib while twisted stitches down the centre of the cable add depth to the pattern. Here the diamonds are off-set to cover the fabric, but if you prefer columns of diamonds, repeat rows 3–16 only for pattern. If you modify the pattern in this way you'll only need a multiple of 12 sts plus 3, rather than 24.

Worked over a multiple of 24 sts plus 3, and 28 rows plus 2

Row 1 (RS): K1, [p1, k1] to end.

Row 2 (WS): [P1, k1] to last st, p1.

Row 3: K1, p1, k1, *p1, k1, p1, 1/1/1 RPC, [p1, k1] 3 times; rep from * to end.

Row 4: *[P1, k1] 3 times, p1, p1tbl, [p1, k1] twice; rep from * to last 3 sts, p1, k1, p1.

Row 5: K1, p1, k1, *p1, k1, 1/1 RPC, k1tbl, 1/1 LPC, [k1, p1] twice, k1; rep from * to end.

Row 6: *[P1, k1] twice, p2, k1, p1tbl, k1, p2, k1; rep from * to

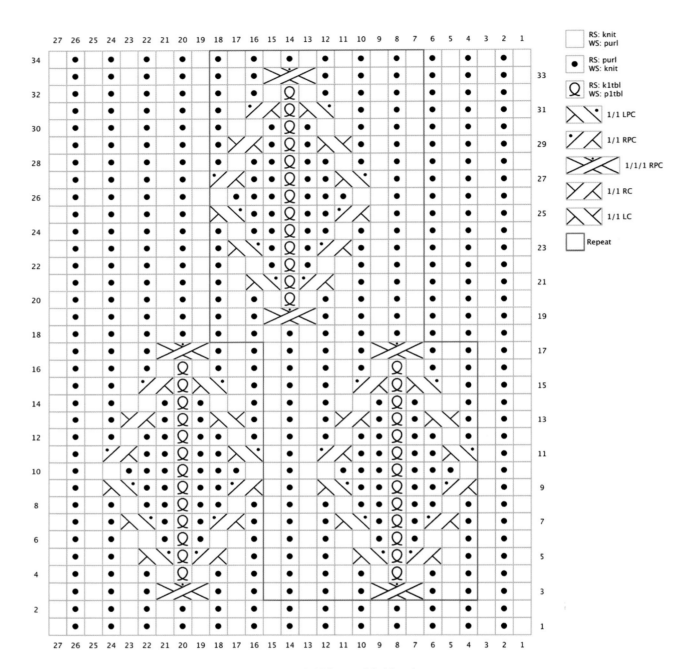

1x1 Diamond Cables chart.

last 3 sts, p1, k1, p1.

Row 7: K1, p1, k1, *p1, 1/1 RPC, p1, k1tbl, p1, 1/1 LPC, [p1, k1] twice; rep from * to end.

Row 8: *[P1, k1] twice, p1, k2, p1tbl, k2, p1, k1; rep from * to last 3 sts, p1, k1, p1.

Row 9: K1, p1, k1, *1/1 RPC, p2, k1tbl, p2, 1/1 LPC, k1, p1, k1; rep from * to end.

Row 10: *P1, k1, p2, k3, p1tbl, k3, p1; rep from * to last 3 sts, p1, k1, p1.

Row 11: K1, p1, k1, *1/1 LPC, p2, k1tbl, p2, 1/1 RPC, k1, p1, k1; rep from * to end.

Row 12: Rep row 8.

Row 13: K1, p1, k1, *p1, 1/1 LC, p1, k1tbl, p1, 1/1 RC, [p1, k1] twice; rep from * to end.

Row 14: Rep row 6.

Row 15: K1, p1, k1, *p1, k1, 1/1 LPC, k1tbl, 1/1 RPC, [k1, p1] twice, k1; rep from * to end.

Row 16: Rep row 4.

Row 17: Rep row 3.

Row 18: Rep row 2.

Row 19: [K1, p1] 3 times, *[k1, p1] 3 times, 1/1/1 RPC, p1, k1, p1; rep from * to last 9 sts, [k1, p1] 4 times, k1.

Row 20: [P1, k1] 4 times, p1, *[k1, p1] twice, p1tbl, [p1, k1] 3 times, p1; rep from * to last 6 sts, [k1, p1] 3 times.

Row 21: [K1, p1] 3 times, *[k1, p1] twice, k1, 1/1 RPC, k1tbl, 1/1 LPC, k1, p1; rep from * to last 9 sts, [k1, p1] 4 times, k1.

Row 22: [P1, k1] 4 times, p1, *k1, p2, k1, p1tbl, k1, p2, [k1, p1] twice; rep from * to last 6 sts, [k1, p1] 3 times.

Row 23: [K1, p1] 3 times, *[k1, p1] twice, 1/1 RPC, p1, k1tbl, p1, 1/1 LPC, p1; rep from * to last 9 sts, [k1, p1] 4 times, k1.

Row 24: [P1, k1] 4 times, p1, *k1, p1, k2, p1tbl, k2, [p1, k1] twice, p; rep from * to last 6 sts, [k1, p1] 3 times.

Row 25: [K1, p1] 3 times, *k1, p1, k1, 1/1 RPC, p2, k1tbl, p2, 1/1 LPC; rep from * to last 9 sts, [k1, p1] 4 times, k1.

Row 26: [P1, k1] 4 times, p1, *p2, k2, p1tbl, k2, p3, k1, p1; rep from * to last 6 sts, [k1, p1] 3 times.

Row 27: [K1, p1] 3 times, *k1, p1, k1, 1/1 LPC, p2, k1tbl, p2, 1/1 RPC; rep from * to last 9 sts, [k1, p1] 4 times, k1.

Row 28: Rep row 24.

Row 29: [K1, p1] 3 times, *[k1, p1] twice, 1/1 LC, p1, k1tbl, p1, 1/1 RC, p1; rep from * to last 9 sts, [k1, p1] 4 times, k1.

Row 30: Rep row 22.

Row 31: *[K1, p1] 3 times, *[k1, p1] twice, k1, 1/1 LPC, k1tbl, 1/1 RPC, k1, p1; rep from * to last 9 sts, [k1, p1] 4 times, k1.

Row 32: Rep row 20.

Row 33: [K1, p1] 3 times, *[k1, p1] 3 times, 1/1/1 RPC, p1, k1,

p1; rep from * to last 9 sts, [k1, p1] 4 times, k1.

Row 34 (WS): Rep row 2.

Rep rows 3–34 for pattern.

Beaded Diamonds

Beads don't have to be saved for lace patterns – they can make a lovely addition to cable patterns as well. Here they've been used to fill in the centre of the diamond and lozenge shapes but, if you prefer to omit them, replace the beaded stitches with p1 for a plain centre or k1 for a moss stitch centre. It's best to use smaller beads for filling the diamonds, as they are placed quite close together – if you are using larger beads, add them more sparingly throughout the diamond centre. A vertical line of twisted stitches separates each panel, but this can be replaced with purl stitches for a plain reverse stocking stitch background.

Worked over a multiple of 18 sts plus 1, and 28 rows

Row 1 (RS): *K1tbl, p4, k2, p2, pb, p2, k2, p4; rep from * to last st, k1tbl.

Row 2 (WS): P1tbl, *k4, p2, k5, p2, k4, p1tbl; rep from * to end.

Row 3: Rep row 1.

Row 4: P1tbl, *k3, p3, k5, p3, k3; rep from * to end.

Row 5: *K1tbl, P3, 2/1 LPC, p2, pb, p2, 2/1 RPC, p3; rep from

Beaded Diamonds stitch pattern.

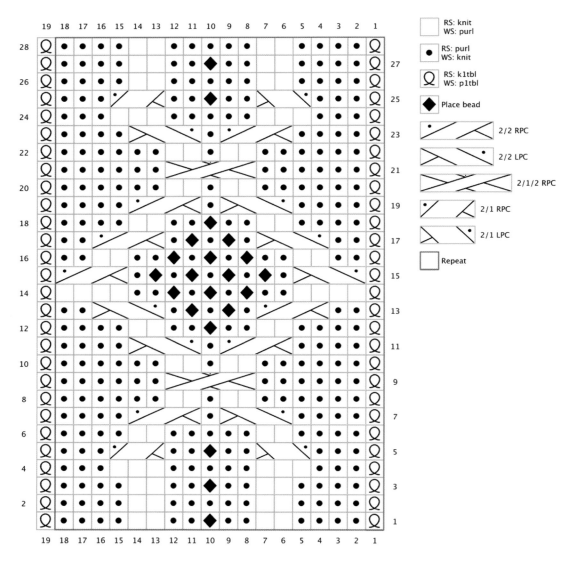

Beaded Diamonds chart.

* to last st, k1tbl.

Row 6: Rep row 2.

Row 7: *K1tbl, p4, 2/2 LPC, p1, 2/2 RPC, p4; rep from * to last st, k1tbl.

Row 8: P1tbl, *k6, p2, k1, p2, k6, p1tbl; rep from * to end.

Row 9: *K1tbl, p6, 2/1/2 RPC, p6; rep from * to last st, k1tbl.

Row 10: Rep row 8.

Row 11: *K1tbl, p4, 2/2 RPC, p1, 2/2 LPC, p4; rep from * to last st, k1tbl.

Row 12: P1tbl, *k4, p2, k2, pb, k2, p2, k4, p1tbl; rep from * to end.

Row 13: *K1tbl, p2, 2/2 RPC, [p1, pb] twice, p1, 2/2 LPC, p2; rep from * to last st, k1tbl.

Row 14: P1tbl, *p4, k2, [pb, k1] twice, pb, k2, p4, p1tbl; rep from * to end.

Row 15: *K1tbl, 2/2 LPC, [p1, pb] 4 times, p1, 2/2 RPC; rep from * to last st, k1tbl.

Row 16: P1tbl, *k2, p2, k2, [pb, k1] 3 times, k1, p2, k2, p1tbl;

rep from * to end.

Row 17: *K1tbl, p2, 2/2 LPC, [p1, pb] twice, p1, 2/2 RPC, p2; rep from * to last st, k1tbl.

Row 18: Rep row 12.

Row 19: *K1tbl, p4, 2/2 LPC, p1, 2/2 RPC, p4; rep from * to last st, k1tbl.

Rows 20–22: Rep rows 8–10.

Row 23: *K1tbl, p4, 2/2 RPC, p1, 2/2 LPC, p4; rep from * to last st, k1tbl.

Rows 24–26: Rep rows 4–6.

Row 27: Rep row 1.

Row 28 (WS): Rep row 2.

Rep rows 1–28 for pattern.

Filigree Columns

Adding twisted stitches to your cable patterns gives a delicate look. Here a bead has been added to the centre of each offset diamond as a focal point, but this can easily be left out if preferred – just purl the stitch instead.

Worked over a multiple of 13 sts and 20 rows

Row 1 (RS): *P2, k1tbl, p1, k1tbl, p3, k1tbl, p1, k1tbl, p2; rep from * to end.

Row 2 (WS): *K2, p1tbl, k1, p1tbl, k3, p1tbl, k1, p1tbl, k2; rep from * to end.

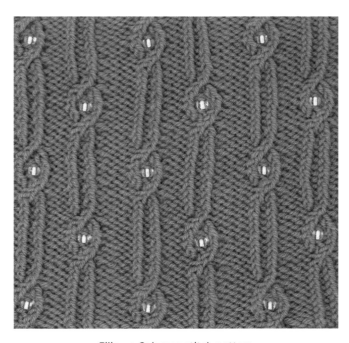

Filigree Columns stitch pattern.

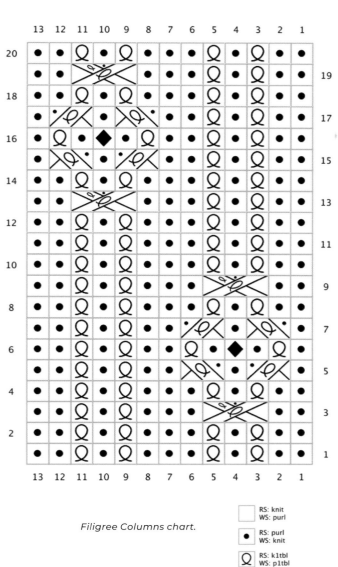

Filigree Columns chart.

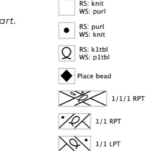

□	RS: knit / WS: purl
●	RS: purl / WS: knit
Ω	RS: k1tbl / WS: p1tbl
◆	Place bead
	1/1/1 RPT
	1/1 RPT
	1/1 LPT

Row 3: *P2, 1/1/1 RPT, p3, k1tbl, p1, k1tbl, p2; rep from * to end.

Row 4: Rep row 2.

Row 5: *P1, 1/1 RPT, p1, 1/1 LPT, p2, k1tbl, p1, k1tbl, p2; rep from * to end.

Row 6: *K2, p1tbl, k1, p1tbl, k2, p1tbl, k1, pb, k1, p1tbl, k1; rep from * to end.

Row 7: *P1, 1/1 LPT, p1, 1/1 RPT, p2, k1tbl, p1, k1tbl, p2; rep from * to end.

Row 8: Rep row 2.

Row 9: Rep row 3.

Row 10: Rep row 2.

Row 11: Rep row 1.

Row 12: Rep row 2.

Row 13: *P2, k1tbl, p1, k1tbl, p3, 1/1/1 RPT, p2; rep from * to end.

Row 14: Rep row 2.

Row 15: *P2, k1tbl, p1, k1tbl, p2, 1/1 RPT, p1, 1/1 LPT, p1; rep from * to end.

Row 16: *K1, p1tbl, k1, pb, k1, p1tbl, k2, p1tbl, k1, p1tbl, k2; rep from * to end.

Row 17: *P2, k1tbl, p1, k1tbl, p2, 1/1 LPT, p1, 1/1 RPT, p1; rep from * to end.

Row 18: Rep row 2.

Row 19: Rep row 13.

Row 20 (WS): *K2, p1tbl, p1, p1tbl, k3, p1tbl, k1, p1tbl, k2; rep from * to end.

Rep rows 1–20 for pattern.

Zig Zag Cables

In this stitch pattern, diagonal cable lines snake back and forth over a background of 2×2 rib for a distinctive zig zag effect. It can be used as an all-over stitch pattern or as 18-st vertical panels over a stocking stitch background.

Worked over a multiple of 16 sts plus 2, and 16 rows plus 2

Row 1 (RS): [K2, p2] to last 2 sts, k2.

Row 2: P2, [k2, p2] to end.

Row 3: *[K2, p2] twice, k2, 2/2 RC, p2; rep from * to last 2 sts, k2.

Row 4: P2, *k2, p6, [k2, p2] twice; rep from * to end.

Row 5: *[K2, p2] twice, 2/2 RPC, k2, p2; rep from * to last 2 sts, k2.

Row 6: Rep row 2.

Row 7: *K2, p2, k2, 2/2 RC, p2, k2, p2; rep from * to last 2 sts, k2.

Zig Zag Cables stitch pattern.

Row 8: P2, *K2, p2, k2, p6, k2, p2; rep from * to end.

Row 9: *K2, p2, 2/2 RPC, [k2, p2] twice; rep from * to last 2 sts, k2.

Row 10: Rep row 2.

Row 11: *K2, p2, 2/2 LC, [k2, p2] twice; rep from * to last 2 sts, k2.

Row 12: Rep row 8.

Row 13: *K2, p2, k2, 2/2 LPC, p2, k2, p2; rep from * to last 2 sts, k2.

Row 14: Rep row 2.

Row 15: *[K2, p2] twice, 2/2 LC, k2, p2; rep from * to last 2 sts, k2.

Row 16: Rep row 4.

Row 17: *[K2, p2] twice, k2, 2/2 LPC, p2; rep from * to last 2 sts, k2.

Row 18 (WS): Rep row 2.

Rep rows 3–18 for pattern.

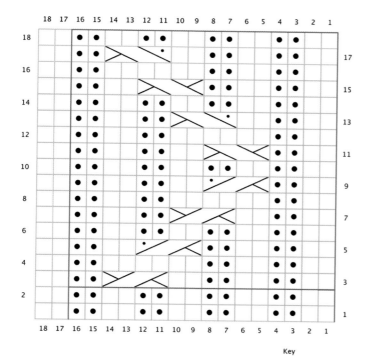

Zig Zag Cables chart.

Key

☐	RS: knit WS: purl
●	RS: purl WS: knit

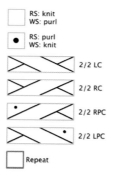

2/2 LC

2/2 RC

2/2 RPC

2/2 LPC

Repeat

Deco Braid

In this fun braided panel, cable lines criss-cross against a background of 2×2 rib so that diagonal lines play with vertical lines in an Art Deco-inspired lattice design. Here the overall emphasis is on straight lines rather than curves, but for a different look try adding an extra curve to the outer rib columns as follows: on row 14, replace the first 5 sts with 'p1, 2/2 LC' and the last 5 sts with '2/2 RC, p1'.

Worked over 24 sts and a multiple of 12 rows plus 11

Row 1 (WS): K1, [p2, k2] 5 times, p2, k1.
Row 2 (RS): P1, 2/2 LC, [k2, p2] 3 times, k2, 2/2 RC, p1.
Row 3: K1, p6, [k2, p2) twice, k2, p6, k1.
Row 4: P1, k2, 2/2 LPC, [p2, k2] twice, p2, 2/2 RPC, k2, p1.
Row 5: Rep row 1.
Row 6: P1, k2, p2, 2/2 LC, k2, p2, k2, 2/2 RC, p2, k2, p1.
Row 7: K1, p2, [k2, p6] twice, k2, p2, k1.
Row 8: P1, k2, p2, k2, 2/2 LPC, p2, 2/2 RPC, k2, p2, k2, p1.
Row 9: Rep row 1.
Row 10: P1, [k2, p2] twice, 2/2/2 RPC, [p2, k2] twice, p1.
Row 11: Rep row 1.
Row 12: P1, k2, p2, k2, 2/2 LC, p2, 2/2 RC, k2, p2, k2, p1.
Row 13: Rep row 7.
Row 14: P1, k2, p2, 2/2 RPC, k2, p2, k2, 2/2 LPC, p2, k2, p1.
Row 15: Rep row 3.
Row 16: Rep row 4.

Deco Braid panel.

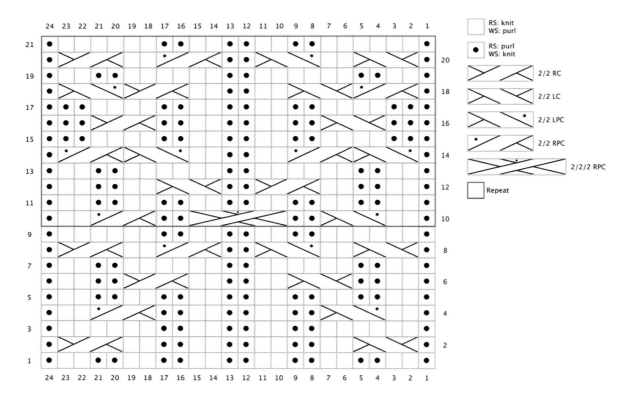

Deco Braid chart.

Row 17: Rep row 1.
Row 18: Rep row 6.
Row 19: Rep row 7.
Row 20: Rep row 8.
Row 21 (WS): Rep row 1.
Rep rows 10–21 for pattern, then complete the pattern by repeating rows 10–11 once more.

Deco Column

This Art Deco-inspired panel of interlocking diamonds contrasts fine 1×1 cables behind larger 2×2 cables over a reverse stocking stitch background. A more complex example of these kinds of cables being used in an Art Deco design can be seen in the Olive sweater.

Worked over 20 sts and 32 rows plus 2

Row 1 (RS): P8, 2/2 RC, p8.

Row 2 (WS): K8, p4, k8.

Rows 3–4: Rep rows 1–2.

Row 5: P6, 2/2 RPC, 2/2 LPC, p6.

Row 6: K6, [p2, k1] twice, p2, k6.

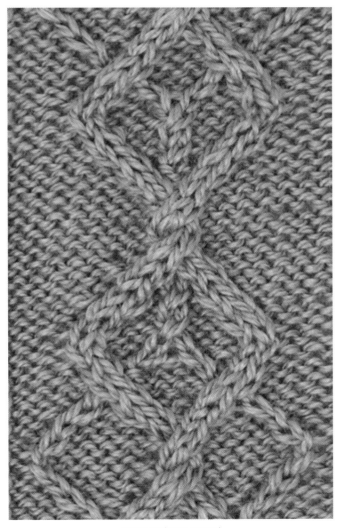

Deco Column panel.

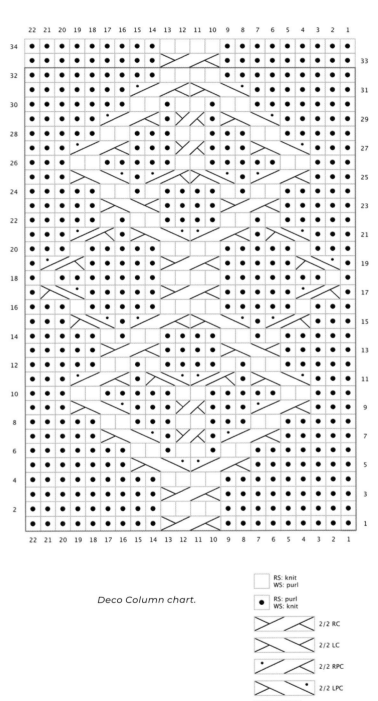

Deco Column chart.

☐	RS: knit / WS: purl
•	RS: purl / WS: knit
⟋⟍	2/2 RC
⟍⟋	2/2 LC
• ⟋	2/2 RPC
⟍ •	2/2 LPC
⟋ •	1/2 LPC
• ⟋	1/2 RPC
⟍⟋	1/1 RC
☐	Repeat

Row 7: P4, 2/2 RPC, p1, 1/1 RC, p1, 2/2 LPC, p4.

Row 8: K4, [p2, k3] twice, p2, k4.

Row 9: P2, 2/2 RPC, p3, 1/1 RC, p3, 2/2 LPC, p2.

Row 10: K2, [p2, k5] twice, p2, k2.

Row 11: P2, 2/2 LPC, p1, 1/2 RPC, 1/2 LPC, p1, 2/2 RPC, p2.

Row 12: K4, p2, k1, p1, k4, p1, k1, p2, k4.

Row 13: P4, 2/2 LPC, p4, 2/2 RPC, p4.

Row 14: K4, p1, k1, p2, k4, p2, k1, p1, k4.

Row 15: P2, 1/2 RPC, p1, 2/2 LPC, 2/2 RPC, p1, 1/2 LPC, p2.

Row 16: K2, p1, k5, p4, k5, p1, k2.

Row 17: 1/2 RPC, p5, 2/2 RC, p5, 1/2 LPC.

Row 18: P1, k7, p4, k7, p1.

Row 19: 1/2 LPC, p5, 2/2 RC, p5, 1/2 RPC.

Row 20: Rep row 16.

Row 21: P2, 1/2 LPC, p1, 2/2 RPC, 2/2 LPC, p1, 1/2 RPC, p2.

Row 22: K4, p1, k1, p2, k4, p2, k1, p1, k4.

Row 23: P4, 2/2 RC, p4, 2/2 LC, p4.

Row 24: Rep row 12.

Row 25: P2, 2/2 RPC, p1, 1/2 LPC, 1/2 RPC, p1, 2/2 LPC, p2.

Row 26: Rep row 10.

Row 27: P2, 2/2 LPC, p3, 1/1 RC, p3, 2/2 RPC, p2.

Row 28: Rep row 8.

Row 29: P4, 2/2 LPC, p1, 1/1 RC, p1, 2/2 RPC, p4.

Row 30: Rep row 6.

Row 31: P6, 2/2 LPC, 2/2 RPC, p6.

Row 32: Rep row 2.

Rep rows 1–32 for pattern, then complete the panel by repeating rows 1–2 once more.

Beaded stitches

These bead designs can be used in a huge variety of ways – add a border to a hem or cuff, work a motif on the back of a fingerless glove or at each end of a plain scarf. Working with beads of different sizes and colours within the same motif can add depth and interest to a design, so don't be afraid to mix it up. Try using larger beads to highlight points where lines change direction or intersect, or to draw greater attention to certain parts of a motif. Beading is one of the easiest areas of knitting in which to experiment, as the gauge is not usually affected and there is no complicated stitch pattern to maintain – use these ideas as a starting point and refer to Chapter 6 to design your own.

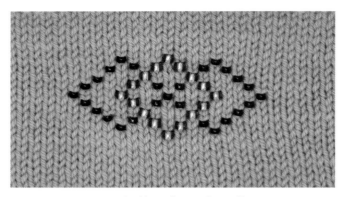

Interlocking Diamonds motif.

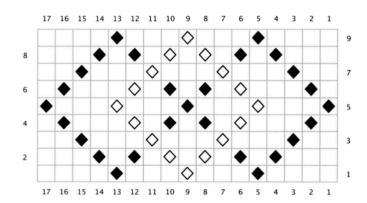

Interlocking Diamonds chart.

Key

	RS: knit WS: purl
◆	Place bead A
◇	Place bead B

Interlocking Diamonds

This single motif is a lovely addition for an area of plain stocking stitch such as a pocket, or it can be repeated across a larger section.

Motif worked over 17 sts and 9 rows

Row 1 (RS): K4, pbA, k3, pbB, k3, pbA, k4.

Row 2 (WS): P3, [pbA, p1] twice, [pbB, p1] twice, pbA, p1, pbA, p3.

Row 3: K2, pbA, [k3, pbB] twice, k3, pbA, k2.

Row 4: P1, pbA, p3, pbB, (p1, pbA] twice, p1, pbB, p3, pbA, p1.

Row 5: [PbA, k3, pbB, k3] twice, pbA.

Row 6: Rep row 4.

Row 7: Rep row 3.

Row 8: Rep row 2.

Row 9 (RS): Rep row 1.

Beaded Zig Zag 1

Beaded but not too feminine, this striking pattern uses larger, paler beads to emphasize the points of the zig zag. Work rows 1–6 once for a hem or edging embellishment or repeat rows 1–6 for an all-over zig zag stripe.

Worked over a multiple of 10 sts plus 1, and 6 rows

Row 1 (RS): [PbB, k9] to last st, pbB.

Row 2 (WS): P1, [pbA, p7, pbA, p1] to end.

Row 3: [K2, pbA, k5, pbA, k1] to last st, k1.

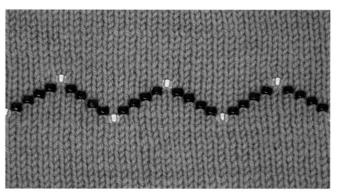

Beaded Zig Zag 1 stitch pattern.

Row 4: P1, *p2, [pbA, p3] twice; rep from * to end.

Row 5: [K4, pbA, k1, pbA, k3] to last st, k1.

Row 6 (WS): P1, [p4, pbB, p5] to end.

Beaded Zig Zag 2

This stitch pattern places smaller zig zags closer together for a more heavily beaded look. Work it once along an edge, or at regular intervals to give stripes with a beaded chevron look. Here two shades of beads have been used, but you could use only one shade of bead, or three for a more complex effect.

Worked over a multiple of 6 sts plus 1, and 10 rows

Row 1 (RS): [PbA, k5] to last st, pbA.

Row 2 (WS): P1, [pbA, p3, pbA, p1] to end.

Row 3: *K2, [pbA, k1] twice; rep from * to last st, k1.

Row 4: PbB, [p2, pbA, p2, pbB] to end.

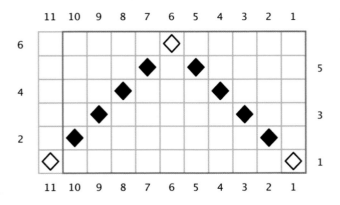

Beaded Zig Zag 1 chart.

RS: knit
WS: purl

Place bead A

Place bead B

Repeat

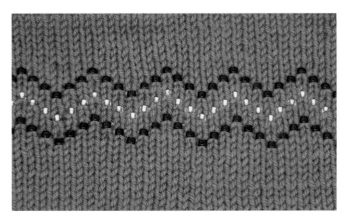

Beaded Zig Zag 2 stitch pattern.

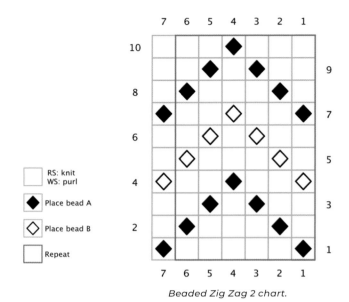

Beaded Zig Zag 2 chart.

Row 6: *P7, [pbB, pbA] twice, pbA, p4; rep from * to end.
Row 7 (RS): *K7, pbB, k8; rep from * to end.

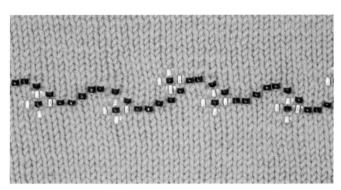

Floral Trim stitch pattern.

Row 5: [K1, pbB, k3, pbB] to last st, k1.
Row 6: P1, *[p1, pbB] twice, p2; rep from * to end.
Row 7: [PbA, k2, pbB, k2] to last st, pbA.
Row 8: Rep row 2.
Row 9: Rep row 3.
Row 10 (WS): P1, [p2, pbA, p3] to end.

Floral Trim

Inspired by pretty floral prints, this delicate design can be repeated in stripes to cover a stocking stitch fabric or worked once to add decoration to an edge. Using different sizes and colours of beads for the flowers gives lots of scope for variation and extra beads can be dotted randomly in the surrounding stocking stitch or added close to the central vine for leaves if desired.

Worked over a multiple of 16 sts and 7 rows
Row 1 (RS): *K12, pbB, k3; rep from * to end.
Row 2 (WS): *P2, [pbB, pbA] twice, pbA, p5, pbB, p3; rep from * to end.
Row 3: *PbA, [pbA, pbB] twice, k3, pbA, k2, pbA, pbB, k3; rep from * to end.
Row 4: *PbA, p2, pbA, p4, pbA, p3, pbB, pbA, p2; rep from * to end.
Row 5: *K3, pbA, k2, pbA, pbB, k5, (pbA) twice, k1; rep from * to end.

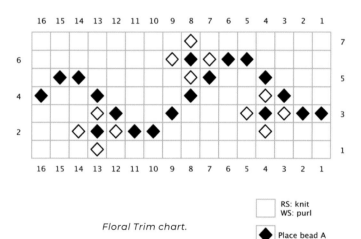

Floral Trim chart.

Beaded Diamonds

These delicate diamonds are beautifully subtle yet eye-catching. Work once along a hem or repeat rows 1–6 several times for the cuff of sleeves or mitts. Leave out the B beads for more open diamonds.

Worked over a multiple of 4 sts plus 3, and 5 rows
Row 1 (RS): K1, [k2, pbA, k1] to last 2 sts, k2.
Row 2 and all WS rows: P2, *[pbA, p1] twice; rep from * to last st, p1.
Row 3: K1, [pbA, k1, pbB, k1] to last 2 sts, pbA, k1.
Row 5: Rep row 1.

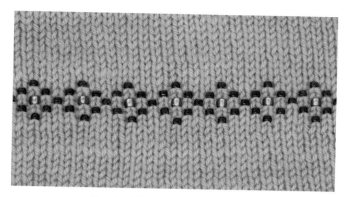

Beaded Diamonds stitch pattern.

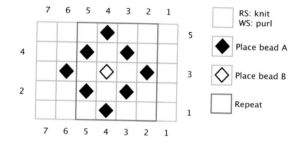

RS: knit
WS: purl

◆ Place bead A

◇ Place bead B

▢ Repeat

Beaded Diamonds chart.

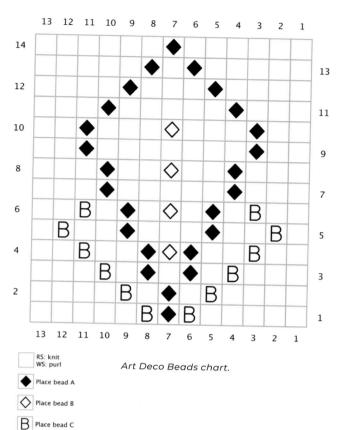

RS: knit
WS: purl

◆ Place bead A

◇ Place bead B

B Place bead C

Art Deco Beads chart.

Art Deco Beads

In this stitch pattern beads are used to outline a classic Art Deco-style motif. Repeat it across a row, or just place a single motif at a focal point of a pattern. Three shades of bead have been used here for a complex effect – alternatively you can work the motif using only one or two kinds of beads.156
Worked over 13 sts and 14 rows
Row 1 (RS): K5, pbC, pbA, pbC, k5.
Row 2 (WS): P4, pbC, p1, pbA, p1, pbC, p4.

Row 3: K3, pbC, k1, [pbA, k1] twice, pbC, k3.
Row 4: P2, pbC, p2, pbA, pbB, pbA, p2, pbC, p2.
Row 5: K1, pbC, k2, pbA, k3, pbA, k2, pbC, k1.
Row 6: P2, pbC, p1, pbA, p1, pbB, p1, pbA, p1, pbC, p2.
Row 7: K3, pbA, k5, pbA, k3.
Row 8: P3, pbA, p2, pbB, p2, pbA, p3.
Row 9: K2, pbA, k7, pbA, k2.
Row 10: P2, pbA, p3, pbB, p3, pbA, p2.
Row 11: Rep row 7.
Row 12: P4, pbA, p3, pbA, p4.
Row 13: K5, pbA, k1, pbA, k5.
Row 14: P6, pbA, p6.

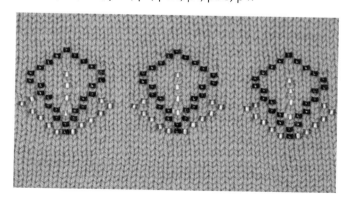

Art Deco Beads motif.

Beaded Arches

This heavily beaded stitch pattern plays with negative space, using a beaded background to emphasize shaped stocking stitch arches. Work rows 1–14 once along an edging or repeat them for an all-over pattern.

Worked over a multiple of 10 sts plus 11, and 14 rows

Row 1 (RS): K1, m1, k3, *s2kpo, k3, m1, pb, m1, k3; rep from * to last 7 sts, s2kpo, k3, m1, k1.

Row 2 (WS): P6, *p4, pb, p5; rep from * to last 5 sts, p5.

Row 3: K2, m1, k2, * s2kpo, k2, m1, pb, k1, pb, m1, k2; rep from * to last 7 sts, s2kpo, k2, m1, k2.

Row 4: P6, *p2, [pb, p1] twice, pb, p3; rep from * to last 5 sts, p5.

Row 5: K3, m1, k1, * s2kpo, k1, m1, [k1, pb] twice, k1, m1, k1; rep from * to last 7 sts, s2kpo, k1, m1, k3.

Row 6: P6, *p1, pb twice, p1, pb, p1, pb twice, p2; rep from * to last 5 sts, p5.

Row 7: K4, m1, * s2kpo, m1, [pb, k1] 3 times, pb, m1; rep from * to last 7 sts, s2kpo, m1, k4.

Row 8: P6, [pb, p1] to last 5 sts, p5.

Row 9: K5, *k2, [pb, k1] 4 times; rep from * to last 6 sts, k6.

Row 10: Rep row 8.

Row 11: K5, *k4, pb, k1, pb, k3; rep from * to last 6 sts, k6.

Row 12: P6, *p1, [pb, p2] 3 times; rep from * to last 5 sts, p5.

Row 13: K5, *[k3, pb] twice, k2; rep from * to last 6 sts, k6.

Row 14: Rep row 2.

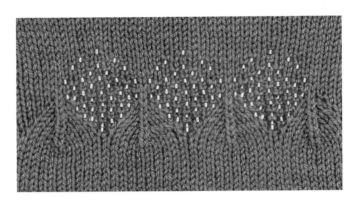

Beaded Arches stitch pattern.

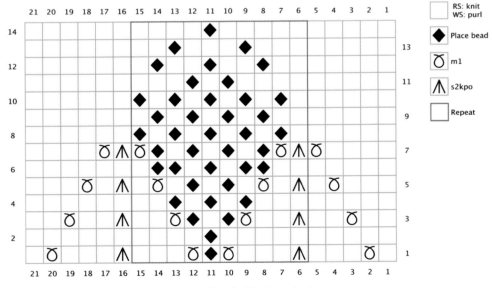

Beaded Arches chart.

Slipped Stitch Beads

This striking stitch pattern is glamorous without being overly feminine, so it's perfect for a stronger, more graphic Art Deco look. It uses elongated slipped stitches and multiple beads to create staggered beaded drops and is easy to customize. Try lengthening the beaded lines by repeating rows 2–3 and rows 6–7 as many times as you like, wrapping the k1e one additional time on rows 1, 5 and 9 for every extra rep of the slip stitch rows and placing extra beads to cover the full length. The precise number of beads needed will depend on the size of bead and the number of slipped stitch rows, but it should cover the full length of the slipped stitch. You can also play with the bead colours to achieve a unique look – try using a blend of shades to give each beaded line an ombre effect, for example.

This stitch pattern uses the following special stitches:

K1e knit 1 elongated: knit the next stitch, wrapping the yarn twice around the right needle tip; drop this extra wrap when you slip the st on the following row.

Pb long place bead long: work as for pb, placing four (or your chosen number) of beads on the crochet hook and sliding them all down onto the stitch.

Worked over a multiple of 8 sts plus 6, and 8 rows plus 1

Row 1 (RS): K3, [k1e, k7] to last 3 sts, k1e, k2.

Row 2 (WS): P2, sl1 pwise wyif, [p7, sl1 pwise wyif] to last 3 sts, p3.

Row 3: K3, [sl1 pwise wyib, k7] to last 3 sts, sl1 pwise wyib, k2.

Row 4: Rep row 2.

Row 5: K3, [pb long, k3, k1e, k3] to last 3 sts, pb long, k2.

Row 6: P3, [p3, sl1 pwise wyif, p4] to last 3 sts, p3.

Row 7: K3, [k4, sl1 pwise wyib, k3] to last 3 sts, k3.

Row 8: Rep row 6.

Row 9 (RS): K3, [k1e, k3, pb long, k3] to last 3 sts, k1e, k2. Rep rows 2–9 for pattern. On the final rep, work k1 instead of k1e on row 9.

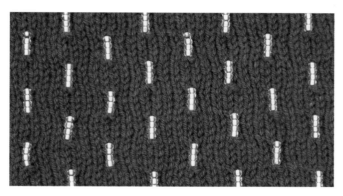

Slipped Stitch Beads stitch pattern.

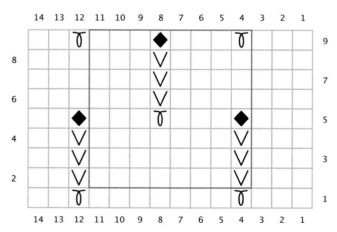

Slipped Stitch Beads chart.

	RS: knit WS: purl
ʊ	k1e
V	RS: sl1 pwise wyib WS: sl1 pwise wyif
◆	pb long
	Repeat

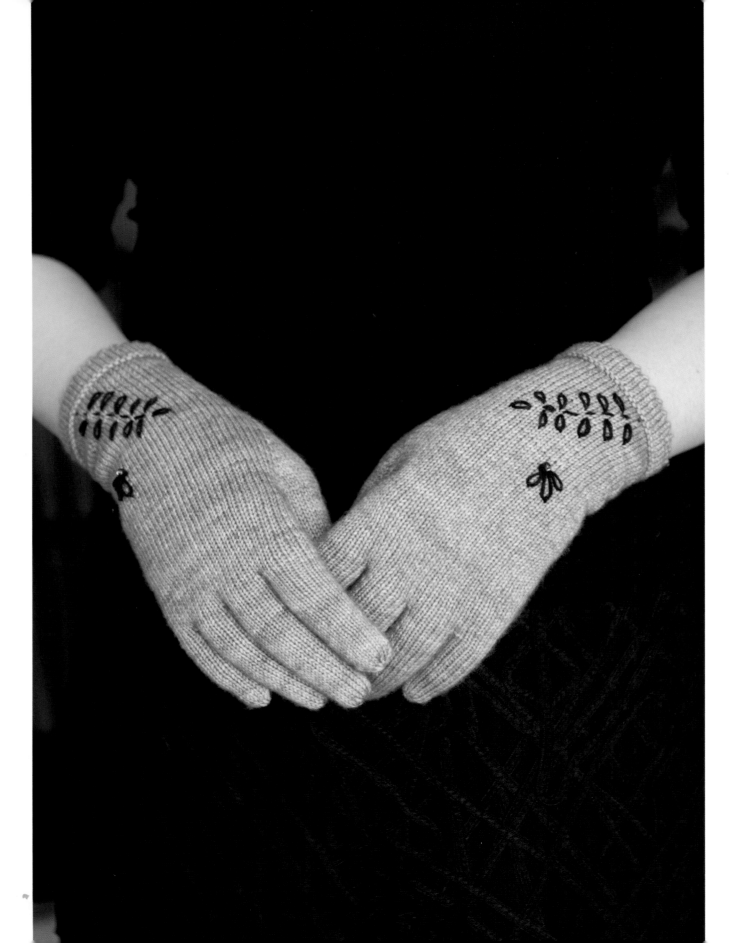

CHAPTER 8

EDGINGS AND HEMS

Stocking stitch has a tendency to curl, so if an edge will not be hidden in a seam it's worth giving some thought to how those edges can be finished and encouraged to lie flat. This can be as simple as adding a few rows of a stitch pattern with an equal distribution of knits and purls such as ribbing, garter stitch or moss stitch (*see* Chapter 7). However, you can also turn the edge of your garment or accessory into a special feature through embellished hems and border stitch patterns. This was a common feature of garments in the 1920s, which would enhance a simple loose silhouette with beading, embroidery or trim at the cuffs, hem and neckline.

Basic hem.

Hems

A sewn hem gives a beautifully neat finish and a pleasant weight to the edge of the piece. A simple hem is nearly invisible, but they can also be complexly patterned and a design feature in their own right. Use these hem ideas as a starting point, then apply your own stitch patterns to give your project a unique touch. Although any knitted edge can be folded over and sewn down into a hem, working a garter stitch ridge on the RS of the fabric produces a fold line and helps give a neat finish.

Basic hem

This simple hem is very subtle and gives a neat, flat edge. Begin by casting on the required number of sts for your knitted piece, then work in stocking stitch until the piece measures the desired length of the hem facing (this is the section that will be folded to the WS and sewn down during finishing).

Decorative hems

Picot hem

Replacing the garter ridge of the hem with an eyelet row of yarnovers will allow you to create a pretty picot edge for your hem.

Cast on the required number of sts and work the hem facing as for the basic hem, ending the facing with a WS row if working flat. On the next row, instead of the garter ridge fold line, work an eyelet fold line by repeating [k2tog, yo] to the end of the row or round. Depending on whether you are working with an odd or even number of sts, end the row with k1 or k2.

Continue as required for your pattern – in this example an equal number of rows have been worked as the hem facing, before adding a garter stitch ridge for extra decoration. Complete the hem in the same way as the Simple Hem, folding the hem facing to the WS along the eyelet row to create a line of picots along the lower edge.

Create the 'foldline' for the hem by creating a garter stitch ridge on the RS of the fabric – this is achieved by working a row of purl sts (if you are working an RS row, or in the round) or working a row of knit sts (if you are working a WS row). Rows/rounds worked after the garter ridge fold will be visible on the finished piece.

Continue with your pattern as required and complete the project. Sew any seams, taking care to match the garter ridge fold line where necessary. Before blocking, complete the hem by turning the hem facing to the WS along the fold line, pinning it in place if necessary.

Neatly sew the hem down on the WS, working in a straight line by carefully matching each cast-on st to the corresponding stitch behind it. Don't pull too tightly as you work, as this may cause the fabric to pucker and prevent the hem from stretching with the rest of the fabric. Complete the hem by sewing the remaining open edge at each side closed.

Picot hem.

Embellished hem.

Garter ridge hem.

Garter ridge hem

Try adding garter ridges to your hems for an interesting effect using clean horizontal lines.

Begin by working a basic hem, until an equal number of rows have been worked before and after the fold line. Work in garter stitch for as many rows as desired to create garter ridges on the RS of the fabric, then continue in your pattern. Complete the hem as normal during finishing.

Embellished hem

Hems can be as eye-catching as you like. This beaded eyelet pattern gives a subtle sparkle and is worked over a multiple of 4 sts plus 1, but you can also embellish your hems by working your choice of bead or lace patterns above them.

Begin by working a basic hem, until an equal number of rows have been worked before and after the fold line, ending with a WS row. Then work a simple eyelet pattern as follows:

Row 1 (RS): K1, [yo, sk2po, yo, k1] to end.

Row 2 (WS): Purl.

Rep rows 1–2 once more, adding a bead to each spine st on Row 1, then continue with your pattern. Complete the hem as normal during finishing, taking care to sew the cast-on edge to the row below the lace pattern.

I-Cord Cast-Off

An i-cord cast-off gives a clean, unfussy finish. It's very neat and smooth so it's a good alternative to a regular cast-off when you want to finish a plain stocking stitch edge. Although it does have more give than a tight cast-off would, it provides a fairly firm edge that will help prevent the stocking stitch from flaring or curling. The thickness of the i-cord edge will depend on how many sts you cast on to work it, indicated by 'X' in the following instructions — most i-cord cast-offs will use 3–5 sts for this.

For an i-cord cast-off, finish your last row then cast on X sts to your left-hand needle tip – these are your i-cord stitches. *K to the last i-cord st (knit [X-1] sts), sl1 kwise, k1 (this is the next live stitch of your last row), psso, slip X sts on right-hand needle back to left-hand needle; rep from * until X sts remain. Cast off or decrease these remaining i-cord sts together and fasten off, leaving a long tail. If working in the round, use this tail to seam the i-cord beginning and end together.

Edgings

Some stitch patterns work particularly well at the edge of your project as they manipulate the fabric into a scalloped edge. Look out for stitch patterns that group stacked decreases and increases separately as distributing the shaping in this way will usually create this effect (by contrast, stitch patterns where the decreases and increases are evenly placed next to each other will usually give a straight edge). This section shows how a simple edging can be used to create a wide range of different looks with the addition of beads – use these ideas as a starting point but don't be afraid to tweak them for your own unique spin on the basic scalloped edge.

Basic edging

This basic edging stacks double decreases on top of each other to create the scalloped shape. It's pretty enough on its own but can also form the basis for more intricate edgings, either through the addition of beads or the use of twisted stitches or purls (*see* Chandelier Lace 1 in Art Deco Stitch Library: Lace Stitches for a more complex version of this stitch pattern). Use yarnovers as increases for a lacy version, as here, or replace them with M1 for a solid edging. You can also add interesting texture by working all WS rows as knit rather than purl.

Basic edging.

Adjusting the size of the basic edging

It's easy to adjust the basic edging for large shells by adding 2 sts and 2 rows at a time. For example, for a slightly larger shell adjust the multiple to 14 sts, and k5 between the increase and decrease on row 3, then continue as set until the increase and decrease are sitting next to each other (you'll work 14 rows of edging, rather than 12, with the final row rep beginning with k6 and ending with k5). Every 2 sts added to the multiple will mean working 1 more st between increase and decrease and will mean the edging takes 2 more rows to complete. Enlarging the basic edging in this way can be useful if you want to fit larger beaded motifs between the scallops.

Worked over a multiple of 12 sts plus 1, and 12 rows
Row 1 (RS): Knit.
Row 2 (WS): Knit.
Row 3: *K1, yo, k4, sk2po, k4, yo; rep from * to last st, k1.
Row 4: Purl.
Row 5: *K2, yo, k3, sk2po, k3, yo, k1; rep from * to last st, k1.
Row 6: Purl.
Row 7: *K3, yo, k2, sk2po, k2, yo, k2; rep from * to last st, k1.
Row 8: Purl.
Row 9: *K4, yo, k1, sk2po, k1, yo, k3; rep from * to last st, k1.
Row 10: Purl.
Row 11: *K5, yo, sk2po, yo, k4; rep from * to last st, k1.
Row 12 (WS): Purl. 171

Beaded Edging 1

This simple variation on the basic edging uses beads to enhance the scalloped shape. Here two shades of beads are used to further accentuate the tip and base of each scallop, but a single shade (or a rainbow!) can be used if preferred.
Worked over a multiple of 12 sts plus 1, and 14 rows
Row 1 (RS): Knit.
Row 2 (WS): Knit.
Row 3: *PbB, yo, k4, sk2po, k4, yo; rep from * to last st, pbB.
Row 4: Purl.

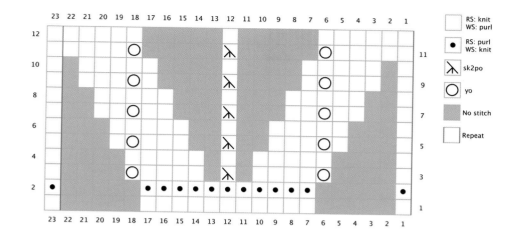

Basic edging chart.

Beaded edging 1.

Row 5: *K1, pbA, yo, k3, sk2po, k3, yo, pbA; rep from * to last st, k1.

Row 6: Purl.

Row 7: *K2, pbA, yo, k2, sk2po, k2, yo, pbA, k1; rep from * to last st, k1.

Row 8: Purl.

Row 9: *K3, pbA, yo, k1, sk2po, k1, yo, pbA, k2; rep from * to last st, k1.

Row 10: Purl.

Row 11: *K4, pbA, yo, sk2po, yo, pbA, k3; rep from * to last

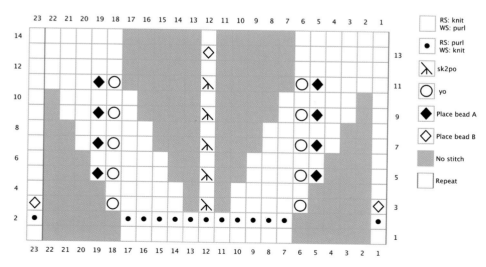

Beaded edging 1 chart.

Beaded edging 2.

M1R; rep from * to last st, k1.
Row 4: P1, *p5, pbB, p6; rep from * to end.
Row 5: *K2, M1L, pbA, k1, pbA, sk2po, pbA, k1, pbA, M1R, k1; rep from * to last st, k1.
Row 6: Rep row 4.
Row 7: *K3, M1L, pbA, k1, sk2po, k1, pbA, M1R, k2; rep from * to last st, k1.
Row 8: Rep row 4.
Row 9: *K4, M1L, pbA, sk2po, pbA, M1R, k3; rep from * to last st, k1.
Row 10: P1, *p4, pbA, pbB, pbA, p5; rep from * to end.
Row 11: *K5, M1L, sk2po, M1R, k4; rep from * to last st, k1.
Row 12 (WS): P1, *p5, pbA, p6; rep from * to end. 175

st, k1.
Row 12: Purl.
Row 13: *K6, pbB, k5; rep from * to last st, k1.
Row 14 (WS): Purl. 173

Beaded Edging 2

This variation uses knitted increases rather than yarnovers to create a solid border, giving the scalloped-shaped edge without a lace look. This edging also adds more beads for extra sparkle and weight.
Worked over a multiple of 12 sts plus 1, and 12 rows
Row 1 (RS): Knit.
Row 2 (WS): Knit.
Row 3: *K1, M1L, [pbA, k1] twice, sk2po, [k1, pbA] twice,

Beaded Edging 3

Make your edging something special by using the spaces between the scallops to show off more complex beaded motifs. Here the straight lines of the decreases have been picked up in the beadwork, making the edging less 'pretty' and more graphic. The beads are the main focus here, so the edging has been toned down by using invisible knitted increases instead of yarnovers for the shaping.
Worked over a multiple of 12 sts plus 1, and 20 rows
Row 1 (RS): Knit.
Row 2 (WS): Knit.
Row 3: *K1, M1L, k4, sk2po, k4, M1R; rep from * to last st, k1.

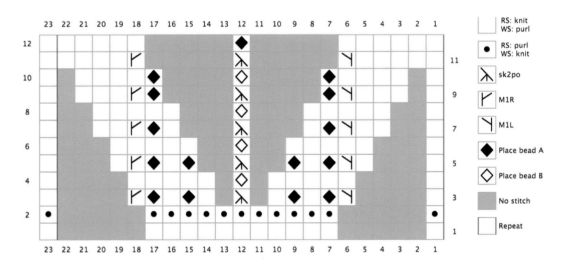

Beaded edging 2 chart.

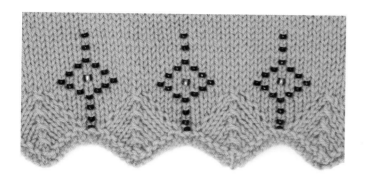

Beaded edging 3.

Row 8: Rep row 4.

Row 9: *K4, M1L, k1, sk2po, k1, M1R, k3; rep from * to last st, k1.

Row 10: Rep row 4.

Row 11: *K1, pbA, k3, M1L, sk2po, M1R, k3, pbA; rep from * to last st, k1.

Row 12: P1, *p1, pbA, p7, pbA, p2; rep from * to end.

Row 13: *PbB, k2, pbA, k5, pbA, k2; rep from * to last st, pbB.

Row 14: Rep row 12.

Row 15: *K1, pbA, k9, pbA; rep from * to last st, k1.

Row 16: Rep row 4.

Row 17: Knit.

Rows 18–19: Rep rows 16–17.

Row 20 (WS): Rep row 4.

Row 4: PbA, [p11, pbA] to end.

Row 5: *K2, M1L, k3, sk2po, k3, M1R, k1; rep from * to last st, k1.

Row 6: Rep row 4.

Row 7: *K3, M1L, k2, sk2po, k2, M1R, k2; rep from * to last st, k1.

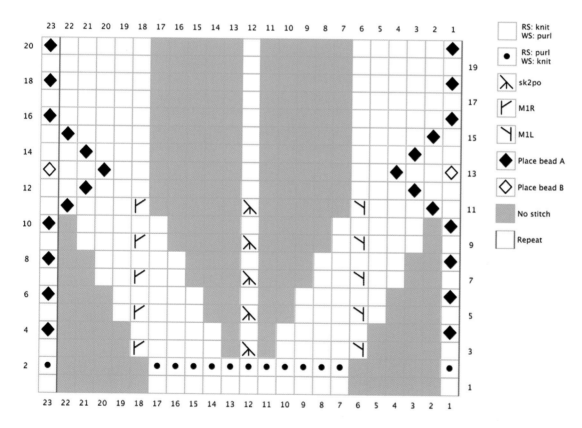

Beaded edging 3 chart.

CHAPTER 9

FINISHING TECHNIQUES

Part of the beauty of hand-knitting is the control you gain over every aspect of your garment, but this can make finishing your project a daunting prospect. This chapter will cover the techniques you need to beautifully finish your handmade garments every time. It's easy to rush through the finishing stage – after all, you're keen to have your project off the needles and into your wardrobe – but try to take your time and enjoy the process. Remember, you are the couturier of your own wardrobe, applying the final touches to your masterpiece!

SEAMS

Although seamless construction is very popular for modern patterns, many vintage patterns were worked flat in pieces and seamed together, much like a sewn garment. Sewing seams can be one of the least appealing aspects of finishing to modern knitters but it's a skill worth practising – seams can add structure and stability to a garment, helping to maintain the close-fitting shape of a 1930s-style sweater.

Here are some tips for seaming success:
- Certain stitches work best for different seams, so make sure you're choosing the right stitch for the job.
- Check your seam on the RS frequently as you go – if you aren't happy with the results, don't be afraid to remove the stitches and make some adjustments or try a different technique.
- If you're new to seaming or struggle to achieve a neat finish, try blocking your pieces flat before seaming, paying particular attention to flattening the edges (*see* the section on blocking at the end of this chapter). Knitted fabric, especially stocking stitch, tends to curl at the edge, which can make sewing the seams more difficult.
- Use pins (it's best to use blunt-tipped pins that are specifically intended for knitted fabrics), locking stitch markers or scraps of waste yarn to connect your seams before you sew them. Even if you just connect the fabric at a few points along a seam, it will allow you to keep an eye on 'the big picture', so that you can ease in any spare fabric

a little at a time as you go.

- Whichever stitch you're using, try to be as consistent as possible, maintaining an even tension and placing stitches an even distance from the edge.
- Learning to read your knitting (see Chapter 5) can be really helpful when it comes to seaming. Ensuring your front and back pieces have an identical number of rows (rather than relying on a work-to measurement) makes aligning the edges for seaming much more straightforward.
- Always use a matching colour for your seams. Usually it's best to use the same yarn for seaming as you did in your project, but if the project yarn was very thick you can slim down the seams by using a thinner yarn in a similar colour. If you're seaming with a delicate yarn, use shorter lengths and work the seams one section at a time to minimize wear and tear on the strand.

Mattress stitch

Mattress stitch is perfect for sewing horizontal seams that can be matched stitch to stitch, such as side and sleeve seams. It gives a nearly invisible finish – just make sure you're matching stitch for stitch as much as possible, and consistently working into the same column of stitches on each side of the seam.

Mattress stitch is worked from the RS of the fabric, so lay the two pieces to be seamed in front of you, RS facing up, with the seam edges together. Begin by connecting the key points of the seam if necessary, using locking stitch markers or pieces of waste yarn – it's usually helpful to at least connect the seam at the end and middle points, but add more markers if you feel you need them. Thread a blunt tapestry needle with a length of yarn that is approximately one and a half times the length of the seam.

Starting at the bottom corner of the right-hand piece, insert your needle from the WS of the fabric through to the RS, one stitch in from the edge. Pull the needle through, leaving a 10–15cm/4–6in tail, then repeat at the bottom corner of the left-hand piece. Insert the needle through both corners once more, then draw on the yarn to pull the corners together.

Take a look at the edges of your pieces – you'll see that between the columns of stitches there is a strand of yarn connecting them. Beginning on the first row of the right-hand piece, insert your needle under this strand and pull the yarn through.

Insert the needle under the corresponding strand on the left-hand piece and pull the yarn through. Now insert your needle under the strand between the stitches on the next row up of the right-hand piece and pull the yarn through. Continue in this way, alternating from side to side, for a couple more stitches.

Pull gently on the yarn – the two edges will 'zip' together into an invisible join. Don't pull too tightly or this will pucker the seam and could break the yarn. Continue in this way, stitching back and forth for a few rows, then pulling on the yarn to close the seam. When the seam is complete, work a couple of extra stitches between the top corners for a strong finish.

Backstitch works best on seams that do not match up evenly stitch for stitch, such as set-in sleeves.

Backstitch

Backstitch creates a firm, strong seam – it's less flexible than mattress stitch, but it works well for seams that need to be hardwearing. It's also the neatest option for setting sleeve caps into armholes, or any other seams that do not match up evenly stitch for stitch.

Backstitch is worked from the WS of the fabric, so begin by holding your two pieces with RS together. Pinning the edges together evenly (or using locking stitch markers or waste yarn) first is a good idea and is especially helpful when setting in sleeves. Thread your needle with a length of yarn approximately three times the length of the seam.

Beginning at the right-hand edge of the seam, insert the needle from front to back through both layers of fabric, then through to the front again slightly to the left of where the needle first entered. Begin working in backstitch along the seam (see Chapter 6 for how to work a backstitch), working through both layers and starting by inserting the needle in the same place it first entered the fabric.

For a neat finish, take care to ensure your stitches remain an even and consistent distance from the edge on both pieces as you sew.

Setting in sleeves using backstitch

To set in sleeves using backstitch, sew your shoulder, side and sleeve seams. Turn the body of your garment inside out so that WS is facing you – the sleeve should be RS out. Place the sleeve inside the armhole so that the RS are together. Align the side and sleeve seam where they meet at the underarm and pin together, then align the shoulder seam with the centre of the top edge of the sleeve cap and pin together. Place further pins around the armhole as desired, so that the fabric is evenly distributed. Beginning at the underarm, use backstitch to seam around the armhole, close to the edge. Try to keep each stitch a consistent distance from the edge of both sleeve and armhole throughout and remove pins as you pass them. Ease the fabrics so that they fit together as you sew along each half of the armhole, making sure that the shoulder seam remains centred at the top of the sleeve cap.

Grafting

Grafting (also known as Kitchener stitch) is used to invisibly join two horizontal sets of live stitches. It's often used to close the gap at the underarm on garments that have been worked without seams, or to join the shoulders – some garments may even be worked in two parts from the sleeve inwards and have the entire centre front and back section grafted together. This technique essentially creates a row of knitting between the two sets of stitches, making it much more flexible than a traditional cast-off seam.

Step 1: Begin with both sets of live stitches held parallel to each other, with WS together – this technique is worked from the RS. Thread a tapestry needle with a length of yarn that is two to three times the length of the seam to be grafted. The knitting needle closest to you is the 'front needle', the needle furthest from you is the 'back needle'.

Step 2: Set up for grafting as follows: insert the threaded tapestry needle purlwise through the first st on the front needle and pull the yarn through, leaving a long tail to weave in later, then insert the tapestry needle knitwise through the first stitch on the back needle and pull through. This set-up step is only worked once.

Step 3: Now begin to graft the stitches together: insert the tapestry needle knitwise through the first stitch on the front needle and slip the stitch off the knitting needle, drawing the yarn through. Insert the tapestry needle purlwise through the next stitch on the front needle and draw through, leaving it on the needle.

Step 4: Insert the tapestry needle purlwise through the first stitch on the back needle and slip the stitch off the knitting needle, drawing the yarn through. Insert the tapestry needle knitwise through the next stitch on the back needle and draw through, leaving it on the needle.

Repeat steps 3 and 4 across the row. Don't worry too much about achieving perfect stitches here, as you'll go back and neaten them at the end. When one stitch remains on each needle, insert the tapestry needle knitwise through the last stitch on the front needle and slip it off the needle, then insert the tapestry needle purlwise through the last stitch on the back needle and slip it off the needle. Now, beginning at the centre of the row, use the tip of a tapestry needle or knitting needle to adjust the tension of each stitch by inserting under the right leg of the stitch and pulling up slightly to tighten, then repeating under the left leg. Work from the centre out, carefully easing out the excess yarn towards the edge.

Weaving in ends

Weaving in your ends is an important final step in finishing your pieces. It should be done after seaming, if applicable. When changing your yarn, casting on or fastening off, always leave an end of at least 10–15cm/4–6in to allow plenty of yarn to weave in. If your project has seams, try to change yarns as close to the seam edge as possible. Tie your ends on the WS of the fabric in a single overhand knot, gently pulling on the ends until the stitches look perfectly even on the RS. It's very important not to a tie a double knot – this can put stress on the yarn and eventually cause it to snap and unravel. Weave in the ends on the WS of the piece, preferably working into the seams if your project has them. Change the direction at least once and take care that the weaving stitches do not show on the RS of the fabric. If the fabric is very delicate or lacy, you may find it easier to hide the ends by splitting the yarn up into individual plies and weaving in each strand separately. Weave in at least 10cm/4in of yarn then block the project before trimming the yarn end close to the fabric.

Picking up stitches

This is a common technique for working neckbands or collars, and button bands, as it helps to stabilize knitted edges and prevent them from stretching out. Here are a few tips to keep in mind for a neat pick-up:
-   It's generally neater to pick up and knit as you go – use just the right needle tip, inserting the tip into the edge, wrapping the yarn around the needle tip and drawing through to create the stitch.
-   Most patterns will give you either an indication of how many stitches to pick up (if the final number of stitches is important), or a ratio to work with, such as 3 sts for every 4 rows, or 1 st for every cast-off st. Try to be consistent in your ratio when picking up. If you are aiming for a spe-

Grafting invisibly joins two sets of stitches. It's often used at the underarms of sweaters worked in the round, like the Josephine sweater.

cific number of stitches, divide the edge to be picked up in half, then half again, placing markers at each point. This makes it easier to track your pick-up progress – you'll want to have a quarter of the total stitches picked up by the first marker, half by the second marker, and so on. You can further divide up the edge if necessary. This prevents you from having to space out the last few sts or work them too close together to achieve the final stitch count.

- If your row gauge is very different to the pattern, you may wish to adjust the total number of stitches you pick up – if you do, double-check if you'll need a particular multiple for your first row after pick-up. For example, if you are picking up stitches for a collar and the following row is '[K2, p2] to end', you'll need to pick up a multiple of 4 sts.
- As you pick up sts, try to insert the needle tip at a consistent distance from the edge throughout. It's best to insert it under a couple of edge strands as a single strand can stretch out. Never split the yarn with the needle tip.
- No matter how careful you are, you're likely to be left with a couple of holes at certain points – these holes are easily closed up on the WS with a short length of yarn, or use your yarn ends to close these holes as you weave them in at the end of your project.

Blocking

Blocking is a simple but important process that is key to a professional-looking finished project. It smooths out any uneven stitches and gives you an opportunity to flatten and manipulate particular areas into the desired shape and size. Some yarns also 'bloom' after washing and blocking, only revealing their true texture after this process (this is why it is so important to wash and block your swatch – see Chapter 5). With lace stitch patterns, blocking is truly magical, opening up the yarnover stitches and revealing the intricacies of the knitting.

Blocking begins with soaking your item – for most hand-knit items with natural fibres, the best way to do this is to soak the piece in a basin of lukewarm water (add some no-rinse wool wash if the item is dirty). Leave it to soak for five to ten minutes – the fibres should be thoroughly saturated. Remove it from the water and gently squeeze out as much water as possible, then roll it up in a clean towel to remove as much remaining water as possible.

Lay your damp piece down on a flat surface with a dry towel – the floor, a bed or table is fine for most projects, but if you will need to stretch the piece firmly make sure to use a surface you can insert pins into. Foam boards are also available for blocking to make this easier.

Begin to gently adjust the shape of the knitted piece, following your pattern measurements. If necessary (for flattened rib or lace patterns) stretch and pin the edges down in place to keep the shape correct.

Leave the piece until it is completely dry – depending on the size of the project this can take one to two days.

Tips for blocking success

- Never use hot water when blocking and try to avoid agitating the knitted fabric as much as possible, to avoid felting the fibres.
- Always support the weight as you remove water from the item – wet knitted fabric can be heavy and easily stretches out of shape.
- Use pins to keep any awkward sections lying flat such as collars or button bands. Always use rust-proof pins.
- You can use a gentle shampoo to wash your knits – just make sure to rinse the piece before removing it from the water.
- Be careful not to overstretch – it's much harder to get a knitted fabric to shrink back in than it is to stretch it out! Try to avoid stretching out waist and cuff ribbing unless specifically told to do so by your pattern.
- Even if you've blocked or pressed your individual pieces before seaming, you should still block the final piece for a neat finish.

Blocking is an important final step in your knitting. It's particularly effective for lace patterns like the Parelli shawl.

CHAPTER 10

JOSEPHINE SWEATER

Josephine is inspired by the distinctive tubular silhouettes of the 1920s, with a simple one-piece, in-the-round construction. Subtle waist shaping gives an elegant fit, and the combination of yoke and raglan shaping in the upper body creates a wide, flattering neckline. Much of the fashion of the 1920s involved simple shapes with embellishments at key focal points. Josephine echoes this style with a deep lace band at the hem and cuffs, while beaded garter ridges add an extra touch of glamour. The yarn is a wool-silk blend, which is perfect for this sweater style, as it allows the fabric to drape well while still keeping its shape.

Measurements
All measurements are finished garment measurements. The sweater is designed to fit with approx. 2.5–7.5cm/1–3" positive ease.

Sizes 1 (2, 3, 4, 5, 6, 7, 8, 9)

a. Bust circumference: 80 (84.5, 88, 94, 100, 106, 109, 115.5, 121.5)cm/31½ (33¾, 35, 37½, 40, 42½, 43¾, 46¼, 48½)"

b. Waist circumference: 76.5 (82.5, 86, 92, 98, 104.5, 107.5, 114, 120)cm/30¼ (32½, 33¾, 36¼, 38¾, 41¼, 42½, 45, 47½)"

c. Hip circumference: 81 (87.5, 90.5, 97, 103, 109.5, 112.5, 118.5, 125)cm/32 (34½, 35¾, 38, 40½, 43, 44½, 46¾, 49¼)"

d. Length to underarm: 33 (33, 33, 34.5, 34.5, 34.5, 35.5, 35.5, 35.5)cm/13 (13, 13, 13½, 13½, 13½, 14, 14, 14)"

e. Sleeve length: 34.5 (35.5, 35.5, 35.5, 37, 37, 38, 38, 38)cm/13½ (14, 14, 14, 14½, 14½, 15, 15, 15)"

f. Upper sleeve circumference: 28 (29, 30, 31, 32, 33, 34, 37, 40)cm/11 (11½, 11¾, 12¼, 12½, 13, 13½, 14½, 15¾)"

g. Lower sleeve circumference: 25 (25, 25, 28, 28, 28, 32, 32, 34.5)cm/9¾ (9¾, 9¾, 11, 11, 11, 12½, 12½, 13½)"

h. Yoke depth (down centre front): 12.5 (13.5, 13.5, 14, 15.5, 16, 16.5, 17, 18)cm/5 (5¼, 5¼, 5½, 6, 6¼, 6½, 6¾, 7)"

i. Neck width: 23 (24, 25.5, 26, 26, 26, 28, 28, 28)cm/9 (9½, 10, 10¼, 10¼, 10¼, 11, 11, 11)"

Making it your own

Josephine offers lots of opportunities for variation:

- For a more authentic 1920s fit, omit the waist shaping completely and work straight to the underarms. Josephine is also easy to shorten into a cropped sweater or lengthen into a tunic – just remember to adjust the yarn requirements accordingly and split any additional length before and after the waist shaping.
- For a more relaxed look, omit the beads by working a plain knit stitch instead of the pb on beaded rows.
- The lace pattern can also be left out – you can work the lace sections in plain stocking stitch, or replace them with a different lace, beaded or even cabled stitch pattern (*see* Chapter 7). To do this, find the closest number that fits both the stitch count given in the pattern and the multiple necessary for your chosen stitch pattern and use this number of stitches for the lace sections. Once the patterned section is complete, increase or decrease the number of stitches evenly during the garter ridge rows to return to the correct stitch count for the remainder of the pattern. Cables in particular will usually result in a tighter tension than lace or stocking stitch, so it's important to check your tension over the new stitch pattern first and make sure it's not too different to the tension listed in the pattern – if it is, you may need to adjust the stitch count, or change to different size needles, when working this section.
- For a truly spectacular piece, work the lace sections in plain stocking stitch when knitting then embellish them later with embroidery (*see* Chapter 6).
- Replace the garter stitch hem and cuffs with a folded hem (*see* Chapter 8).

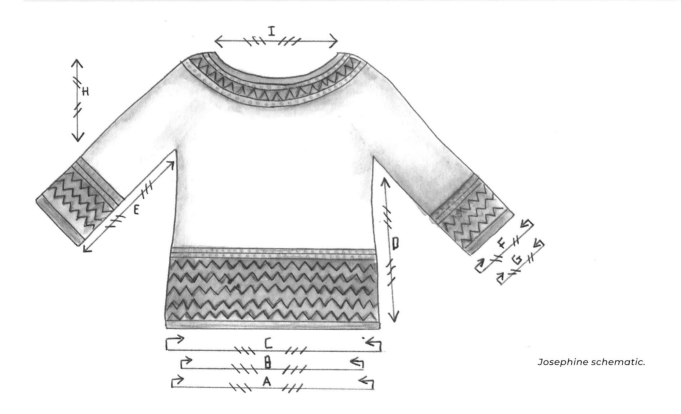

Josephine schematic.

Materials
1000 (1072, 1104, 1212, 1275, 1334, 1448, 1527, 1651)m/1093 (1173, 1208, 1326, 1395, 1459, 1584, 1670, 1806)yds of 4-ply/fingering weight yarn
Shown in:
Quince & Co Tern (4-ply/fingering weight; 75% American wool, 25% silk; 202 m/221 yds per 50g/1¾oz skein)
Shade: 415 Dusk; 5 (6, 6, 7, 7, 7, 8, 8, 9) skeins
540 (564, 580, 620, 640, 656, 692, 712, 756) size 6 seed beads

Needles
3.25mm/US 3 circular needles, of an appropriate length for the size you are working, and needles suitable for working small circumferences in the round

2.75mm/US 2 circular needles, 60cm/24" length, for neckband

0.8mm crochet hook (or hook small enough to fit through chosen beads)
Tapestry needle for seaming

Gauge
26 sts & 38 rows to 10cm/4", measured over stocking stitch in the round with 3.25mm needles, after blocking.
Always check your gauge before beginning and adjust your needle size if necessary.

Special stitches
Place bead (pb): Work to the stitch to be beaded, place bead on crochet hook then place stitch on hook. Draw bead down the hook and onto the stitch; return beaded stitch to left needle and knit it (*see* Chapter 6 for tutorial).

Written instructions for chart
Worked over a multiple of 8 sts and 6 rounds
Row 1: *K1, yo, ssk, k3, k2tog, yo; rep from * to end.
Row 2: Knit.
Row 3: *K2, yo, ssk, k1, k2tog, yo, k1; rep from * to end.

Row 4: Knit.
Row 5: *K3, yo, sk2po, yo, k2; rep from * to end.
Row 6: Knit.

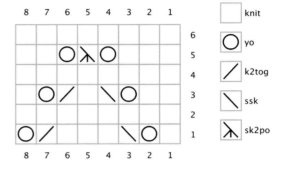

Josephine chart.

Many 1920s sweaters were knit in simple stitches with bands of decoration. Josephine's elegant wide neckline is enhanced with an angular lace pattern surrounded by rows of sparkling beads and garter ridges.

Pattern

Body

Cast on 208 (224, 232, 248, 264, 280, 288, 304, 320) sts. Knit 1 row. PM and join to work in the round. Note that beg of round marker is at right 'side seam'.

Round 1: Purl.
Round 2: Knit.

Repeat rounds 1–2 a further 2 (2, 2, 3, 3, 3, 3, 4, 4) times. Commence lace pattern as follows:

Next round: Work row 1 of Lace Chart, working 8-st rep 26 (28, 29, 31, 33, 35, 36, 38, 40) times across the round.

Continue to work through the chart as set until 5 (5, 5, 5, 5, 6, 6, 6, 7) reps of the Lace Chart have been worked in total. Now work the beaded garter stripe as follows:

Round 1: Purl.
Round 2–3: Knit.
Round 4: [K1, pb] to end.

Rep rounds 1–4 once more.

Next round: Purl.
Next round: K104 (112, 116, 124, 132, 140, 144, 152, 160), PM, k to end.

Continue in St st and commence waist shaping as follows:

Next round (Dec): *K1, ssk, k to 3 sts before marker, k2tog, k1; rep from * once more. 4 sts dec

Work in St st for 9 rounds.

Repeat Dec round on next and foll tenth round. 196 (212, 220, 236, 252, 268, 276, 292, 308) sts

Work in St st for 21 rounds.

Next round (Inc): *K1, m1, k to 1 st before marker, m1, k1; rep from * once more. 4 sts inc

Work in St st for 11 rounds.

Rep Inc round once more. 204 (220, 228, 244, 260, 276, 284, 300, 316) sts

Work straight in St st until piece measures 33 (33, 33, 34.5, 34.5, 34.5, 35.5, 35.5, 35.5)cm/13 (13, 13, 13½, 13½, 13½, 14, 14, 14)" from cast-on edge.

Next round: K to marker, remove marker, k5 (6, 6, 7, 8, 9, 9, 10, 11), place last 10 (12, 12, 14, 16, 18, 18, 20, 22) sts worked on holder or waste yarn, k to end, remove beg of round marker, k5 (6, 6, 7, 8, 9, 9, 10, 11), place last 10 (12, 12, 14, 16, 18, 18, 20, 22) sts worked on hold.

Place all rem sts on hold separately and set aside.

Sleeves

Using needles suitable for working small circumferences in the round, cast on 64 (64, 64, 72, 72, 72, 80, 80, 88) sts. Knit 1 row. PM and join to work in the round.

Round 1: Purl.
Round 2: Knit.

Repeat rounds 1–2 a further 2 (2, 2, 3, 3, 3, 3, 4, 4) times. Commence lace pattern as follows:

Next round: Work row 1 of Lace Chart, working 8-st rep 8 (8, 8, 9, 9, 9, 10, 10, 11) times across the round.

Continue to work through the chart as set until 4 (4, 4, 4, 4, 5, 5, 5, 6) reps of the Lace Chart have been worked in total. Now work the beaded garter stripe as follows:

Round 1: Purl.
Round 2–3: Knit.
Round 4: [K1, pb] to end.

Rep rounds 1–4 once more.

Next round: Purl.

Work in St st for 11 rounds.

Next round (Inc): K1, m1, k to last st, m1, k1. 2 sts inc

Rep last 12 rounds a further 3 (4, 5, 3, 4, 5, 3, 6, 6) times. 72 (74, 76, 80, 82, 84, 88, 94, 102) sts

Continue in St st until sleeve measures 34.5 (35.5, 35.5, 35.5, 37, 37, 38, 38, 38)cm/13½ (14, 14, 14, 14½, 14½, 15, 15, 15)". Place 5 (6, 6, 7, 8, 9, 9, 10, 11) sts on each side of beg of round marker on hold for underarm. Place 62 (62, 64, 66, 66, 66, 70, 74, 80) rem Sleeve sts on hold separately and set aside. Repeat for second sleeve.

Yoke

Join the sleeves and body to work the yoke as follows:

Next round: Leaving all underarm sts on hold, k across first held 92 (98, 102, 108, 114, 120, 124, 130, 136) sts of body for back, PM, k across held 62 (62, 64, 66, 66, 66, 70, 74, 80) Left Sleeve sts, PM, k across held 92 (98, 102, 108, 114, 120, 124, 130, 136) front sts, PM, k across held 62 (62, 64, 66, 66, 66, 70, 74, 80) Right Sleeve sts, PM for beg of round. 308 (320, 332, 348, 360, 372, 388, 408, 432) sts

Knit 4 rounds, slipping markers as you pass them.

Raglan Dec round: K1, k2tog, k to 3 sts before marker, ssk, k1; rep from * three times. 8 sts dec

Knit 1 round.

Rep last 2 rounds a further 7 (8, 8, 9, 9, 10, 11, 12, 14) times.

244 (248, 260, 268, 280, 284, 292, 304, 312) sts
Remove all markers except the beg of round marker.
Yoke Dec round 1: K4 (0, 4, 4, 0, 4, 4, 0, 0), [k6, k2tog] to end. 214 (217, 228, 235, 245, 249, 256, 266, 273) sts
Knit 1 round.
Purl 1 round.
Yoke Dec round 2: K to end and dec 6 (1, 4, 3, 5, 9, 8, 10, 9) sts evenly across the round. 208 (216, 224, 232, 240, 240, 248, 256, 264) sts
Knit 1 round.
Next round: [K1, pb] to end.
Purl 1 round.
Knit 1 round.
Commence lace pattern as follows:
Next round: Work row 1 of Lace Chart, working 8-st rep 26 (27, 28, 29, 30, 30, 31, 32, 33) times across the round.
Continue to work through the chart as set until 1 (1, 1, 1, 2, 2, 2, 2, 2) reps of the Lace Chart have been worked in total.
Yoke Dec round 3: [P24 (25, 26, 27, 13, 13, 29, 14, 31), p2tog] to end. 200 (208, 216, 224, 224, 224, 240, 240, 256) sts
Knit 2 rounds.

Next round: [K1, pb] to end.
Yoke Dec round 4: [P6, p2tog] to end. 175 (182, 189, 196, 196, 196, 210, 210, 224) sts
Knit 1 round.
Yoke Dec round 5: [K5, k2tog] to end. 150 (156, 162, 168, 168, 168, 180, 180, 192) sts
Knit 1 round.
Yoke Dec round 6: [K4, k2tog] to end. 125 (130, 135, 140, 140, 140, 150, 150, 160) sts
Knit 1 round.
Change to smaller circular needles and work neckband as foll:
Round 1: Purl.
Round 2: Knit.
Rep rounds 1–2 twice. Cast off purlwise.

Finishing

Graft together the two sets of held sts at each underarm (*see* Chapter 9). Weave in all ends and block to measurements, gently opening up the lace pattern. You may wish to pin down the garter stitch edges at the hem so that they block flat.

CHAPTER 11

PARELLI SHAWL

The perfect accessory for day or night, Parelli is a delicate laceweight shawl inspired by evening shawls from the 1920s. It mixes a traditional leaf lace pattern with garter stitch stripes in an easy sideways construction, for a modern twist on the traditional triangular shawl. Beads are placed on the 'spine stitches' between yarnovers on the lace sections to give a glamorous look for evening but can also be left out for a more casual shawl.

Measurements
Sizes 1 (2)
a. Length (top edge): 152.5 (193)cm/60 (76)"
b. Depth (along short edge): 96.5 (126)cm/38 (50)"

Materials
620 (1020)m/674 (1116)yds of 2 ply/laceweight yarn
896 (1440) size 8 seed beads (optional)

Making it your own

Use Parelli as the basis for a shawl worked in your own preferred pattern. Follow the increase structure as set out by the pattern and work garter stitch sections until you reach the required number of stitches to work your chosen stitch pattern (see Chapter 7). During patterned sections, incorporate increased stitches into your stitch pattern (or, if in doubt, simply work them in stocking stitch).

Shown in:
Size 1
Debonnaire Yarns Squeal Lace (2 ply/laceweight yarn; 65% superwash merino, 20% silk, 15% yak; 800m/875yds per 100g/3½oz skein)
Shade: Burnished Gold; 1 skein

Size 2
West Yorkshire Spinners Exquisite (2 ply/laceweight; 80% Falkland wool, 20% mulberry silk; 800m/875yds per 100g/3½oz skein)
Shade: Rose 560; 2 skeins

Needles
3.25mm/US 3 knitting needles

Gauge
29 sts & 38 rows to 10cm/4", measured over garter stitch with 3.25mm needles, after firm blocking.
Always check your gauge before beginning and adjust your needle size if necessary.

Special stitches
Place bead (pb): Work to the stitch to be beaded, place bead on crochet hook then place stitch on hook. Draw bead down the hook and onto the stitch; return beaded stitch to left needle and knit it (*see* Chapter 6 for tutorial).

Written instructions for chart
Row 1 and every WS row: K2, p to last 2 sts, k2.
Row 2 (RS): Kfb, k1, k2tog, *p2, yo, pb, yo, p2, ssk, k5, k2tog; rep from * to last 5 sts, p2, yo, pb, k2. 1 st inc
Row 4: Kfb, k1, k2tog, *p2, k1, yo, pb, yo, k1, p2, ssk, k3, k2tog; rep from * to last 6 sts, p2, k1, yo, pb, k2. 1 st inc
Row 6: Kfb, k1, k2tog, *p2, k2, yo, pb, yo, k2, p2, ssk, k1, k2tog; rep from * to last 7 sts, p2, k2, yo, pb, k2. 1 st inc
Row 8: Kfb, k1, k2tog, *p2, k3, yo, pb, yo, k3, p2, sk2po; rep from * to last 8 sts, p2, k3, yo, pb, k2. 1 st inc
Row 10: Kfb, k2, pb, yo, *p2, ssk, k5, k2tog, p2, yo, pb, yo; rep from * to last 9 sts, p2, ssk, k5. 1 st inc
Row 12: Kfb, k3, pb, yo, k1, *p2, ssk, k3, k2tog, p2, k1, yo, pb, yo, k1; rep from * to last 8 sts, p2, ssk, k4. 1 st inc
Row 14: Kfb, k4, pb, yo, k2, *p2, ssk, k1, k2tog, p2, k2, yo, pb,

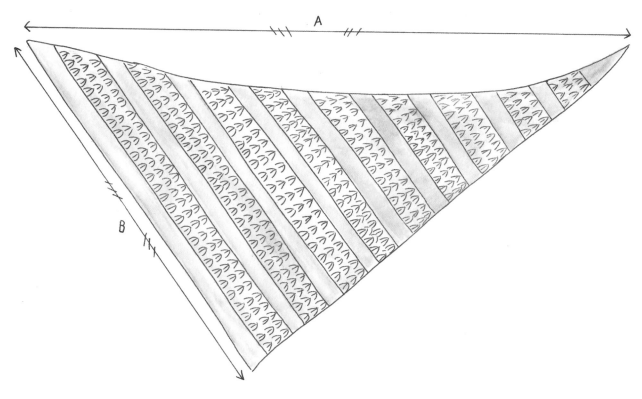

Parelli schematic.

Parelli looks equally lovely with or without beads and fits easily into a modern wardrobe.

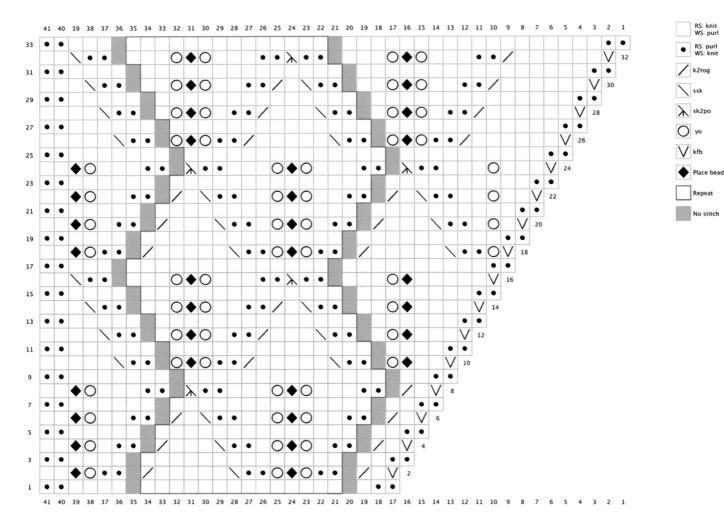

Parelli chart.

yo, k2; rep from * to last 7 sts, p2, ssk, k3. 1 st inc

Row 16: Kfb, k5, pb, yo, k3, *p2, sk2po, p2, k3, yo, pb, yo, k3; rep from * to last 6 sts, p2, ssk, k2. 1 st inc

Row 18: Kfb, *yo, p2, ssk, k5, k2tog, p2, yo, pb; rep from * to last 2 sts, k2. 1 st inc

Row 20: Kfb, k1, *yo, k1, p2, ssk, k3, k2tog, p2, k1, yo, pb; rep from * to last 2 sts, k2. 1 st inc

Row 22: Kfb, k2, *yo, k2, p2, ssk, k1, k2tog, p2, k2, yo, pb; rep from * to last 2 sts, k2. 1 st inc

Row 24: Kfb, k3, *yo, k3, p2, sk2po, p2, k3, yo, pb; rep from

* to last 2 sts, k2. 1 st inc

Row 26: Kfb, k6, *k2tog, p2, yo, pb, yo, p2, ssk, k5; rep from * to end. 1 st inc

Row 28: Kfb, k6, *k2tog, p2, k1, yo, pb, yo, k1, p2, ssk, k3; rep from * to last st, k1. 1 st inc

Row 30: Kfb, k6, *k2tog, p2, k2, yo, pb, yo, k2, p2, ssk, k1; rep from * to last 2 sts, k2. 1 st inc

Row 32: Kfb, k6, k2tog, p2, k3, yo, pb, yo, k3, *p2, sk2po, p2, k3, yo, pb, yo, k3; rep from * to last 6 sts, p2, ssk, k2. 1 st inc

Row 33 (WS): K2, p to last 2 sts, k2.

Pattern notes

This shawl is worked from side-to-side, beginning at one corner to create an asymmetric shape. The beads are optional – simply knit the stitch without beading it if you prefer. The size is also easily adjusted by continuing to repeat sections 1 and 2 until the shawl reaches the desired size, ending with a Section 1. The pink shawl pictured is a size 2 with beads, the gold shawl is a size 1 without beads.

Pattern

Set-up 1 – Garter

Cast on 1 st.

Row 1 (RS): Kfb. 2 sts

Row 2 (WS): Knit.

Row 3 (RS): Kfb, k to end. 1 st inc

Rows 2–3 establish garter stitch and shawl shaping; unless otherwise specified, continue to work as set in garter stitch throughout, increasing 1 st with a kfb at beginning of every RS row. Place locking stitch marker to mark RS of shawl if desired.

Work in garter stitch as set until there are 23 sts on needle, ending with an RS row.

Set-up 2 – Chart

Next row (WS): Work row 1 of chart to end.
Continue to work as set to end of chart. 16 sts inc; 39 sts

Section 1 – Garter Stitch

Beginning with an RS row and increasing at beg of every RS rows as set, work in garter stitch pattern for a further 23 rows, ending with an RS row. 12 sts inc; 51 sts

Section 2 – Chart

Next row (WS): Work row 1 of chart, working 14-st rep as many times as necessary.
Continue to work as set to end of chart. 16 sts inc; 67 sts

Repeat sections 1–2 a further 5 (7) times, then section 1 only once more. 219 (275) sts
Cast off loosely kwise on WS.

Finishing

Weave in ends and block to measurements.

CHAPTER 12

OLIVE SWEATER

Combining a modern silhouette with a Deco-influenced stitch pattern is a great way to give a project a subtle vintage flair. Olive is a classic, wearable sweater covered in large geometric cables inspired by Art Deco motifs. The fit is relaxed and worn slightly loose with a touch of flattering waist shaping. Worked in a lightweight wool yarn, this cosy sweater can be dressed up or down as part of a modern or vintage inspired outfit – pair it with skinny jeans and boots or tucked into a skirt with a silk scarf at the neck.

Measurements

All measurements are finished garment measurements. The sweater is designed to fit with zero ease.

Sizes 1 (2, 3, 4, 5, 6, 7, 8, 9)

a. **Bust circumference:** 76.5 (81.5, 86.5, 91.5, 96.5, 101.5, 106.5, 111.5, 116.5)cm/30 (32, 34, 36, 38, 40, 42, 44, 46)"

b. **Waist circumference:** 72.5 (77.5, 82.5, 87.5, 92.5, 98, 103, 108, 113)cm/28½ (30½, 32½, 34½, 36½, 40½, 42½, 44½)"

Making it your own

- For a boxier fit, omit the waist shaping, working straight to the armholes.
- The sweater is designed to be slightly cropped but the length is easily adjusted. If you are adding significant length and including the waist shaping, divide the extra length in two and work half of it before the waist shaping begins to maintain the correct fit. Remember to purchase extra yarn.
- The shape and construction of this sweater is simple, so if you're feeling confident try replacing the Cable Panels with other Art Deco-influenced stitch patterns. Just make sure your replacement panel measures approximately the same as the original (see Gauge) – remember you can always add extra reverse stocking stitches to the sides of your panel to reach the correct measurement.

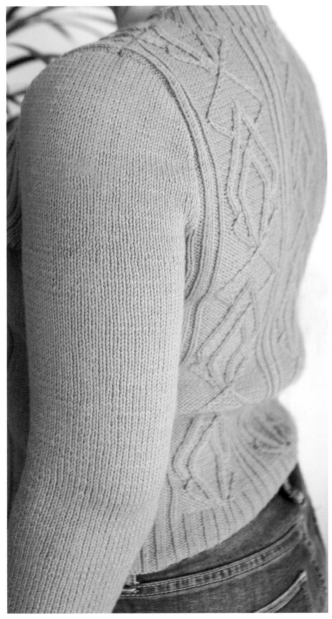

Olive combines an Art Deco-inspired fabric with a classic, easy-to-wear shape.

33, 34.5, 36.5)cm/10 (10¼, 10½, 11, 12, 12½, 13, 13½, 14½)"

f. **Lower sleeve circumference:** 18 (18, 18, 19.5, 19.5, 21, 21, 22.5, 22.5)cm/7 (7, 7, 7¾, 7¾, 8¼, 8¼, 9, 9)"

g. **Sleeve length:** 43 (43, 43, 43, 43, 44.5, 44.5, 45.5, 45.5)cm/17 (17, 17, 17, 17, 17½, 17½, 18, 18)"

h. **Back neck width:** 16 (16, 18, 18, 18.5, 19, 19, 19, 19)cm/6¼ (6¼, 7, 7, 7¼, 7½, 7½, 7½, 7½)"

Materials

1135 (1247, 1253, 1320, 1412, 1502, 1583, 1689, 1780) m/1241 (1365, 1371, 1445, 1545, 1643, 1732, 1848, 1948) yds of 4-ply/fingering weight yarn

Shown in:

Quince & Co Finch (4-ply/fingering weight; 100% American

Cable stitches can be used to create angular lines and diagonal motifs, which makes them perfect for Art Deco motifs.

c. **Length to underarm:** 30cm/12"

d. **Armhole depth:** 16 (16.5, 17, 18, 18.5, 19, 19.5, 20, 21)cm/6¼ (6½, 6¾, 7, 7¼, 7½, 7¾, 8, 8¼)"

e. **Upper sleeve circumference:** 25 (26, 26.5, 28, 30.5, 32,

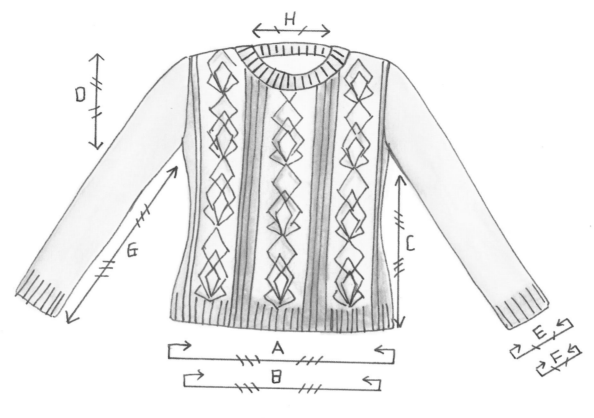

Olive schematic.

Wool; 202m/221yds per 50g/1¾oz skein)
Shade: Honey; 6 (7, 7, 7, 8, 8, 8, 9, 9) skeins

Needles/Notions
3.25mm/US 3 knitting needles
2.75mm/US 2 knitting needles
2.75mm/US 2 circular needles, 40cm/16" length (or preferred needles for working small circumferences in the round), for neckband
Cable needle
Tapestry needle for seaming
8 stitch markers
Waste yarn or stitch holder

Gauge
26 sts & 38 rows to 10cm/4", measured over stocking stitch with 3.25mm needles, after blocking.
33-st Cable Panel measures 7cm/2¾" wide, after blocking. Always check your gauge before beginning and adjust your needle size if necessary.

Special stitches
1/1 LPC: Slip 1 st to cable needle and hold at front of work, p1, k1 from cable needle.
1/2 RC: Slip 2 sts to cable needle and hold at back of work, k1, k2 from cable needle.
1/2 LC: Slip 1 st to cable needle and hold at front of work, k2, k1 from cable needle.

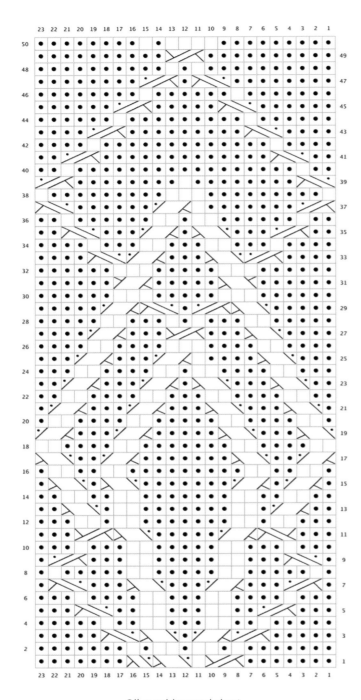

Olive cable panel chart.

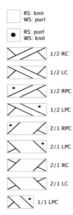

	RS: knit WS: purl
●	RS: purl WS: knit
	1/2 RC
	1/2 LC
	1/2 RPC
	1/2 LPC
	2/1 RPC
	2/1 LPC
	2/1 RC
	2/1 LC
	1/1 LPC

1/2 RPC: Slip 2 sts to cable needle and hold at back of work, k1, p2 from cable needle.

1/2 LPC: Slip 1 st to cable needle and hold at front of work, p2, k1 from cable needle.

2/1 RPC: Slip 1 st to cable needle and hold at back of work, k2, p1 from cable needle.

2/1 LPC: Slip 2 sts to cable needle and hold at front of work, p1, k2 from cable needle.

Rib Panel

Worked over 10 (10, 10, 10, 14, 14, 14, 18, 18) sts and 2 rows

Row 1 (RS): [P1, k1] 1 (1, 1, 1, 2, 2, 2, 3, 3) times, p2, k2, p2, [k1, p1] 1 (1, 1, 1, 2, 2, 2, 3, 3) times.

Row 2 (WS): [K1, p1] 1 (1, 1, 1, 2, 2, 2, 3, 3) times, k2, p2, k2, [p1, k1] 1 (1, 1, 1, 2, 2, 2, 3, 3) times.

Rep rows 1–2 for Rib Panel.

Written instructions for chart

Worked over 23 sts and 50 rows

Row 1 (RS): P7, 1/2 RC, k1, 2/1 LPC, 1/1 LPC, p7.

Row 2 (WS): K7, p1, [k1, p2] twice, k1, p1, k7.

Row 3: P5, 1/2 RPC, 2/1 RPC, p1, 2/1 LPC, 1/2 LPC, p5.

Row 4: K5, p1, k2, p2, k3, p2, k2, p1, k5.
Row 5: P3, 1/2 RPC, p2, k2, p3, k2, p2, 1/2 LPC, p3.
Row 6: K3, p1, k4, p2, k3, p2, k4, p1, k3.
Row 7: P1, 1/2 RPC, p3, 2/1 RPC, p3, 2/1 LPC, p3, 1/2 LPC, p1.
Row 8: K1, p1, [k5, p2] twice, k5, p1, k1.
Row 9: P1, 1/2 LPC, p3, k2, p5, k2, p3, 1/2 RPC, p1.
Row 10: K3, p1, k3, p2, k5, p2, k3, p1, k3.
Row 11: P3, 1/2 LC, 2/1 RPC, p5, 2/1 LPC, 1/2 RC, p3.
Row 12: K3, p2, k1, p2, k7, p2, k1, p2, k3.
Row 13: P2, 2/1 RPC, p1, k2, p7, k2, p1, 2/1 LPC, p2.
Row 14: [K2, p2] twice, k7, [p2, k2] twice.
Row 15: [P1, 2/1 RPC] twice, p7, [2/1 LPC, p1] twice.
Row 16: K1, p2, k2, p2, k9, p2, k2, p2, k1.
Row 17: 2/1 RPC, p2, 2/1 LPC, p7, 2/1 RPC, p2, 2/1 LPC.
Row 18: P2, k4, p2, k7, p2, k4, p2.
Row 19: 2/1 LPC, p3, 2/1 LPC, p5, 2/1 RPC, p3, 2/1 RPC.
Row 20: K1, p2, k4, p2, k5, p2, k4, p2, k1.
Row 21: P1, [2/1 LPC, p3] twice, 2/1 RPC, p3, 2/1 RPC, p1.
Row 22: K2, p2, k4, p2, k3, p2, k4, p2, k2.
Row 23: P2, 2/1 LPC, p3, 2/1 LPC, p1, 2/1 RPC, p3, 2/1 RPC, p2.
Row 24: K3, p2, k4, p2, k1, p2, k4, p2, k3.
Row 25: P3, 2/1 LPC, p4, k1, [2/1 RPC, p3] twice.
Row 26: K4, p2, k4, p3, k4, p2, k4.
Row 27: P4, 2/1 LPC, p3, 1/2 RC, p3, 2/1 RPC, p4.
Row 28: K5, p2, k3, p1, k1, p1, k3, p2, k5.
Row 29: P5, 2/1 LPC, 1/2 RPC, p1, 1/2 LPC, 2/1 RPC, p5.
Row 30: K6, p3, k5, p3, k6.
Row 31: P6, 2/1 LPC, p5, 2/1 RPC, p6.
Row 32: Rep row 30.
Row 33: P4, 1/2 RPC, 2/1 LPC, p3, 2/1 RPC, 1/2 LPC, p4.
Row 34: K4, p1, [k3, p2] twice, k3, p1, k4.
Row 35: P2, 1/2 RPC, p3, 2/1 LPC, p1, 2/1 RPC, p3, 1/2 LPC, p2.
Row 36: K2, p1, k6, p2, k1, p2, k6, p1, k2.
Row 37: 1/2 RPC, p7, k1, 2/1 RPC, p6, 1/2 LPC.
Row 38: P1, k9, p3, k9, p1.
Row 39: 1/2 LPC, p8, k1, p8, 1/2 RPC.
Row 40: K2, p1, k17, p1, k2.
Row 41: P2, 1/2 LPC, p13, 1/2 RPC, p2.
Row 42: K4, p1, k13, p1, k4.
Row 43: P4, 1/2 LPC, p9, 1/2 RPC, p4.
Row 44: K6, p1, k9, p1, k6.
Row 45: P6, 1/2 LPC, p5, 1/2 RPC, p6.
Row 46: K8, p1, k6, p1, k7.
Row 47: P8, 1/2 LPC, p1, 1/2 RPC, p8.

Row 48: K10, p1, k1, p1, k10.
Row 49: P10, 1/2 RC, p10.
Row 50 (WS): K8, p1, k1, p4, k9.

Pattern

Back

Using smaller needles, cast on 121 (129, 137, 145, 153, 161, 169, 177, 185) sts.

Rib row 1 (RS): K2, [p2, k2] 1 (2, 3, 4, 3, 4, 5, 4, 5) times, PM, *work row 1 of Rib Panel, PM, p1, [k2, p2] twice, k1, p1, k1, p2, k1, p1, k2, p2, k2, p1, PM; rep from * twice more, work row 1 of Rib Panel, PM, k2, [p2, k2] to end.

Rib row 2 (WS): P2, [k2, p2] to marker, SM, *work row 2 of Rib Panel, SM, k1, p2, k2, p2, k1, p1, k2, p1, k1, p1, [k2, p2] twice, SM; rep from * twice more, work row 2 of Rib Panel once, SM, p2, [k2, p2] to end.

Rep Rib rows 1–2 until piece measures 5cm/2" from cast on, ending with a WS row.

Change to larger needles.

Next row (RS): K to marker, SM, *work row 1 of Rib Panel, SM, work row 1 of Cable Panel (working from chart or written instructions), SM; rep from * twice more, work row 1 of Rib Panel, SM, k to end.

Next row (WS): P to marker, SM, *work row 2 of Rib Panel, SM, work next row of Cable Panel, SM; rep from * twice more, work row 2 of Rib Panel, SM, p to end.

Continue in patt as est, working St st at each edge, repeating rows 1–2 of Rib Panel and working through Cable Panel, until piece measures 9cm/3½", ending with a WS row.

Next row (Dec)(RS): K1, ssk, patt to last 3 sts, k2tog, k1. 2 sts dec

Continue as est and rep Dec row every eighth row twice more. 115 (123, 131, 139, 147, 155, 163, 171, 179) sts

Continue straight in patt for a further 15 rows.

Next row (Inc) (RS): K1, m1, patt to last st, m1, k1. 2 sts inc

Continue as est and rep Inc row every eighth row twice more. 121 (129, 137, 145, 153, 161, 169, 177, 185) sts

Continue straight in patt until piece measures 30cm/12" from cast-on or desired length to armhole, ending with a WS row.

Shape armhole

Note: As you work the following armhole shaping, keep the est rib and cable patt correct. The decreases will eventually move into the Rib Panel at each side, so remove the outermost stitch markers when necessary.

Cast off 5 (6, 6, 9, 9, 11, 11, 11, 12) sts at beg of next 2 rows. 111 (117, 125, 127, 135, 139, 147, 155, 161) sts

Next row (RS): Ssk, patt to last 2 sts, k2tog. 2 sts dec

Next row (WS): P2tog, patt to last 2 sts, ssp. 2 sts dec

Working decreases as set by last two rows, dec 1 st at each end of every row a further 1 (3, 5, 5, 5, 5, 5, 7, 7) times then every RS row 1 (2, 2, 3, 3, 4, 4, 4, 4) times. 103 (103, 107, 107, 115, 117, 125, 129, 135) sts **

Work straight, maintaining Rib and Cable Panels as established, until armhole measures 16 (16.5, 17, 18, 18.5, 19, 19.5, 20, 21)cm/6¼ (6½, 6¾, 7, 7¼, 7½, 7¾, 8, 8¼)", ending with a WS row.

Note: As you work the foll shoulder shaping, keep est patt correct where possible – if unable to complete a cable stitch, work those sts in rev St st instead.

Next row (RS): Patt across 24 (24, 24, 24, 27, 27, 31, 33, 35) sts, k2tog and turn, leaving remaining sts on hold. 25 (25, 25, 25, 28, 28, 32, 34, 36) sts

Work each side of back neck separately.

Right neck

Row 1 (WS): P2tog, patt to end. 24 (24, 24, 24, 27, 27, 31, 33, 35) sts

Row 2 (RS): Cast off 6 (6, 6, 6, 7, 7, 8, 8, 8) sts, patt to last 2 sts, k2tog. 17 (17, 17, 17, 19, 19, 22, 24, 26) sts

Row 3: Patt to end.

Row 4: Cast off 6 (6, 6, 6, 7, 7, 8, 8, 8) sts, patt to end. 11 (11, 11, 11, 12, 12, 14, 16, 18) sts

Rep rows 3–4 once more.

Cast off remaining 5 (5, 5, 5, 5, 5, 6, 8, 10) sts.

Left neck

With RS facing, leave first 51 (51, 55, 55, 57, 59, 59, 59, 61) sts on hold for back neck and rejoin yarn to rem sts.

Row 1 (RS): Ssk, patt to end. 25 (25, 25, 25, 28, 28, 32, 34, 36) sts

Row 2 (WS): Patt to last 2 sts, p2tog. 24 (24, 24, 24, 27, 27, 31, 33, 35) sts

Row 3: Ssk, patt to end. 23 (23, 23, 23, 26, 26, 30, 32, 34) sts

Row 4: Cast off 6 (6, 6, 6, 7, 7, 8, 8, 8) sts, patt to end. 17 (17, 17, 17, 19, 19, 22, 24, 26) sts

Row 5: Patt to end.

Rep rows 4–5 once then row 4 only once more.

Cast off rem 5 (5, 5, 5, 5, 5, 6, 8, 10) sts.

Front

Work as for Back to **. 103 (103, 107, 107, 115, 117, 125, 129, 135) sts

Work straight, maintaining Rib and Cable Panels as est, until armhole measures 9 (9.5, 10, 11, 11.5, 12, 12.5, 13.5, 14)cm/3½ (3¾, 4, 4¼, 4½, 4½, 4¾, 5, 5)", ending with a WS row.

Note: As you work the foll shoulder shaping, keep est patt correct where possible – if unable to complete a cable stitch, work those sts in rev St st instead.

Next row (RS): Patt across 34 (34, 35, 35, 39, 39, 44, 45, 48) sts, k3tog and turn, leaving rem sts on hold. 35 (35, 36, 36, 40, 40, 45, 46, 49) sts

Work each side of front neck separately.

Left neck

Next row (WS): P3tog, patt to end. 2 sts dec

Next row (RS): Patt to last 2 sts, k3tog. 2 sts dec

Next row (WS): P2tog, patt to end. 1 st dec

Next row (RS): Patt to last 2 sts, k2tog. 1 st dec

Working decreases as set by last two rows, continue in patt and dec 1 st at neck edge of every row 4 (4, 5, 5, 6, 6, 7, 6, 7) times then every RS row only 2 times. 23 (23, 23, 23, 26, 26, 30, 32, 34) sts

Work straight, maintaining Rib and Cable Panels as est, until armhole measures same as back armhole to shoulder, ending with a WS row.

Shape shoulder as follows:

Row 1 (RS): Cast off 6 (6, 6, 6, 7, 7, 8, 8, 8) sts, patt to end. 17 (17, 17, 17, 19, 19, 22, 24, 26) sts

Row 2: Patt to end.

Rep rows 1–2 once more then row 1 only once.

Cast off rem 5 (5, 5, 5, 5, 5, 6, 8, 10) sts.

Right neck

With RS facing, leave first 29 (29, 31, 31, 31, 31, 31, 33, 33) sts on hold for front neck and rejoin yarn to rem 37 (37, 38, 38, 42, 42, 47, 48, 51) sts.

Next row (RS): Sssk, patt to end. 35 (35, 36, 36, 40, 40, 45, 46, 49) sts

Next row (WS): Patt to last 2 sts, sssp. 2 sts dec

Next row (RS): Sssk, patt to end. 2 sts dec

Next row (WS): Patt to last 2 sts, ssp. 1 st dec

Next row (RS): Ssk, patt to end. 1 st dec

Working decreases as set by last two rows, continue in patt and dec 1 st at neck edge of every row 4 (4, 5, 5, 6, 6, 7, 6, 7) times then every RS row only 2 times. 23 (23, 23, 23, 26, 26, 30, 32, 34) sts

Work straight, maintaining Rib and Cable Panels as est, until armhole measures same as back armhole to shoulder, ending with an RS row.

Shape shoulder as follows:

Row 1 (WS): Cast off 6 (6, 6, 6, 7, 7, 8, 8, 8) sts, patt to end. 17 (17, 17, 17, 19, 19, 22, 24, 26) sts

Row 2: Patt to end.

Rep rows 4–5 once then row 1 only once more.

Cast off rem 5 (5, 5, 5, 5, 5, 6, 8, 10) sts.

Sleeves

Using smaller needles, cast on 46 (46, 46, 50, 50, 54, 54, 58, 58) sts.

Rib Row 1 (RS): K2, [p2, k2] to end.

Rib Row 2 (WS): P2, [k2, p2] to end.

Rep Rib rows 1–2 until piece measures 5cm/2" from cast-on, ending with a WS row.

Change to larger needles.

Next row (Inc)(RS): K1, m1, k to last st, m1, k1. 2 sts inc

Continue in St st and rep Inc row every eighth row 0 (0, 0, 1, 7, 8, 10, 10, 13) times then every tenth row 8 (9, 10, 9, 6, 5, 4, 4, 4) times. 64 (66, 68, 72, 78, 82, 84, 88, 94) sts

Continue straight in St st until sleeve measures 43 (43, 43, 43, 43, 44.5, 44.5, 45.5, 45.5)cm/17 (17, 17, 17, 17, 17½, 17½, 18, 18)" or desired length to underarm.

Shape sleeve cap:

Cast off 5 (6, 6, 9, 9, 11, 11, 11, 12) sts at beg of next 2 rows. 54 (54, 56, 54, 60, 60, 62, 66, 70) sts

Next row (RS): Ssk, k to last 2 sts, k2tog. 2 sts dec

Next row (WS): P2tog, p to last 2 sts, ssp. 2 sts dec

Working decreases as set by last two rows, continue in St st and dec 1 st at each end of next row, then every RS row 1 (2, 2, 2, 2, 2, 2, 2, 3) times, then every fourth row 7 (8, 8, 9, 8, 9, 10, 10, 10) times, then every RS row 3 (2, 3, 1, 3, 3, 2, 2, 2) times, then every row 5 (3, 3, 3, 5, 3, 3, 5, 5) times. 16 (18, 18, 18, 18, 20, 22, 22, 24) sts

Cast off 4 sts at beg of next 2 rows. Cast off remaining 8 (10, 10, 10, 10, 12, 14, 14, 16) sts.

Finishing

Sew the shoulder seams using backstitch, being careful to match the rib and cable stitches at front and back.

Using mattress stitch, seam the side and sleeve seams, then set the sleeves into the armholes using backstitch.

Neckband

With RS facing, using smaller circular needles and beg at left shoulder seam, pick up and knit 24 (24, 24, 24, 24, 26, 26, 26, 28) sts down left side of front neck, knit across held 29 (29, 31, 31, 31, 31, 31, 33, 33) sts front neck sts, pick up and knit 24 (24, 23, 23, 24, 25, 25, 26, 27) sts up right side of front neck, pick up and knit 6 sts down right side of back neck, knit across held 51 (51, 55, 55, 57, 59, 59, 59, 61) back neck sts, pick up and knit 6 (6, 5, 5, 6, 5, 5, 6, 5) sts up left side of back neck. 140 (140, 144, 144, 148, 152, 152, 156, 160) sts

Round 1: [K2, p2] to end.

Rep Round 1 until neckband measures 2.5cm/1".

Cast off loosely in rib.

Weave in all ends and block to measurements.

CHAPTER 13

FRANCES SWEATER

One of the most charming features of 1930s knitting patterns is the 'party' sweater, a glamorous piece which was often knit in rayon (the popular 'artificial silk') and saved for evening wear. Knit in a deep red wool-silk blend yarn, Frances aims to resurrect the party sweater for the modern knitter. It begins with a deep 1×1 ribbed waistband for a nipped-in look before gradually increasing to the bust, following the popular close-fitting silhouette that emerged during the 1930s. A beaded mesh section at the neck gives the illusion of a wide V-neck and echoes the clever neckline effects and embellishments that were popular during the 1930s, as well as adding plenty of sparkle for that candle-lit party.

Measurements
All measurements are finished garment measurements. The sweater is designed to fit with 0–5cm/0–2" negative ease. Sizes 1 (2, 3, 4, 5, 6, 7, 8, 9)
a. Bust circumference: 75 (80, 85, 90, 95, 100, 105, 110, 115)cm/30 (32, 34, 36, 38, 40, 42, 44, 46)"
b. Waist circumference: 63 (68.5, 73, 77, 83, 87, 93, 97, 103)cm/25¼ (27½, 29¼, 31, 33¼, 35, 37¼, 39, 41¼)"

c. Side seam length: 26.5 (28, 28, 28, 29, 29, 29, 30.5, 30.5)cm/10½ (11, 11, 11, 11½, 11½, 11½, 12, 12)"
d. Armhole depth: 16.5 (17, 18, 18.5, 19.5, 20.5, 21, 21.5, 22.5)cm/6½ (6¾, 7, 7¼, 7¾, 8, 8¼, 8½, 8¾)"
e. Sleeve length: 32 (32, 33, 33, 33, 34, 34, 34, 34)cm/12½ (12½, 13, 13, 13, 13½, 13½, 13½, 13½)"
f. Upper sleeve circumference: 23.5 (24.5, 26, 28, 29.5, 30.5, 31.5, 33.5, 35)cm/9½ (9¾, 10¼, 11¼, 11¾, 12¼, 12½, 13½, 14)"
g. Lower sleeve circumference: 18.5 (19.5, 20, 21.5, 22, 23, 24.5, 26.5, 28)cm/7½ (7¾, 8, 8½, 8¾, 9¼, 9¾, 10½, 11¼)"
h. Neck opening width: 20 (20, 20.5, 20.5, 20, 20.5, 20, 21.5, 23)cm/8 (8, 8¼, 8, 8¼, 8, 8½, 9¼)"

Materials
830 (900, 960, 1010, 1120, 1184, 1260, 1366, 1440)m/907 (984, 1049, 1105, 1224, 1294, 1376, 1494, 1575)yds of 4-ply/fingering weight yarn
Shown in:
Fyberspates Scrumptious 4 Ply/Sport Superwash (4-ply/fingering weight; 45% silk, 55% superwash merino; 365m/399

Making it your own

- The beads at the neckline offer plenty of scope for variation. Omit them for a plain mesh, or experiment with different colours – use a mix of shades across the mesh or create an ombre effect by beginning with one shade of bead and gradually beginning to use new shades as you move up the mesh.
- This sweater can also be pared back completely into a plain 1930s 'template' pattern by ignoring the mesh pattern at the neck and working the front the same as the back to the front neck, then following the shaping instructions only. This makes it perfect for experimenting with other stitch patterns and techniques. Try knitting a plain sweater then embroidering a pretty floral pattern around the neck, working a beaded pattern around the waist above the rib, or adding an all-over stitch pattern to the pieces – just remember to double check that your tension in the new stitch pattern matches that listed in the pattern.
- For a more bloused effect (another popular 1930s silhouette), work all of the bust increases just above the waist ribbing by increasing 16 (16, 16, 18, 16, 18, 16, 18, 16) sts on the first stocking stitch row of the body when working the front and back, then work straight to the armholes. It's a good idea to purchase extra yarn if you change the shaping in this way.

Frances features a delicate bead and lace detail at the neckline for a sparkling evening look. For a more casual sweater, simply omit the beads.

yds per 100g/3½oz skein)
Shade: 301 Cherry; 3 (3, 3, 3, 4, 4, 4, 4, 5) skeins
Approx. 120 (130, 140, 150, 160, 170, 180, 190, 200) size 8 seed beads

Needles
2.75mm/US 2 knitting needles
0.8mm crochet hook (or hook small enough to fit through chosen beads)
Tapestry needle for seaming

Gauge
28 sts & 40 rows to 10cm/4", measured over stocking stitch with 2.75mm needles, after blocking.
Always check your gauge before beginning and adjust your needle size if necessary.

Special stitches
Place bead (pb): Work to the stitch to be beaded, place bead on crochet hook then place stitch on hook. Draw bead down the hook and onto the stitch; return beaded stitch to left needle and knit it (*see* Chapter 6 for tutorial).
Pfb and Pbf: In order to achieve a neat, mirrored effect at the neckline, the purl increase on each side of the neckline is worked slightly differently, as follows:
Pfb: Purl into the front and back of the yo (2 sts worked into yo).
Pbf: Purl into the back of the yo and slip off left needle. Insert left needle from front to back under strand between stitch just worked and next stitch, and purl it (2 sts worked into yo).

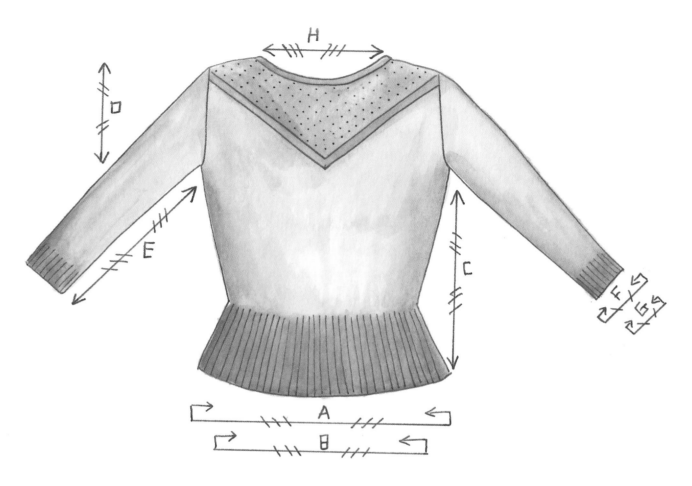

Frances schematic.

Written instructions for charts

Bead Pattern Swatch Chart

Worked over a multiple of 4 sts plus 4 and 8 rows

Row 1 (RS): K2, [yo, sk2po, yo, pb] to last 2 sts, k2.

Row 2 and all WS rows: Purl.

Row 3: K2, [k2tog, yo] to last 2 sts, k2.

Row 5: K1, k2tog, [yo, pb, yo, sk2po] to last st, yo, k1.

Row 7: Rep row 3.

Row 8 (WS): Purl.

Bead Pattern Chart

Row 1 (RS): K2tog, yo, ssk. 3 sts

Row 2 (WS): Ssp, (k1, p1, k1) into yo, p2tog. 5 sts

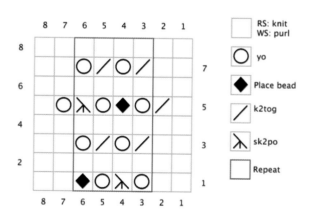

Frances Bead Pattern Swatch chart.

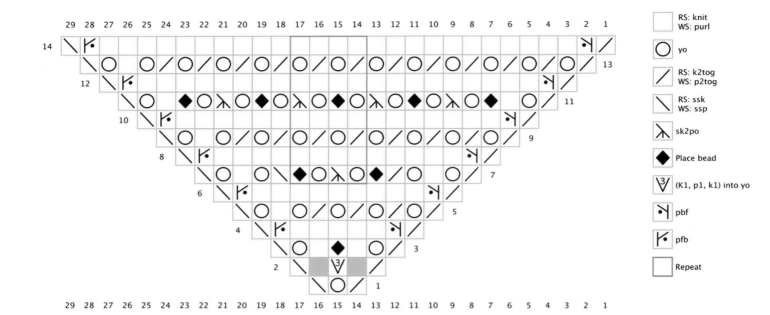

Frances Bead Pattern chart.

Row 3: K2tog, yo, k1, pb, k1, yo, ssk. 6 sts
Row 4: Ssp, pfb, p5, pbf, p2tog. 9 sts
Row 5: [K2tog, yo] 4 times, k1, yo, ssk. 11 sts
Row 6: Ssp, pfb, p9, pbf, p2tog. 13 sts
Row 7: K2tog, yo, k1, yo, k2tog, pb, [yo, sk2po, yo, pb] to last 3 sts before decrease, ssk, yo, k1, yo, ssk. 2 sts added from body
Row 8: Ssp, pfb, p to last st before decrease, pbf, p2tog. 2 sts added
Row 9: [K2tog, yo] to last st before decrease, k1, yo, ssk. 2 sts added
Row 10: Ssp, pfb, p to last st before decrease, pbf, p2tog. 2 sts added
Row 11: K2tog, yo, k1, pb, yo, sk2po, [yo, pb, yo, sk2po] to last 2 sts before decrease, yo, pb, k1, yo, ssk. 2 sts added
Row 12: Ssp, pfb, p to last st before decrease, pbf, p2tog. 2 sts added

Row 13: Rep row 9. 2 sts added
Row 14: Ssp, pfb, p to last st before decrease, pbf, p2tog. 2 sts added
Rep rows 7–14 as indicated.

Pattern notes

Take the time to practise the Bead Pattern before working the front neckline, as you will need to keep the pattern correct as you work the neck shaping and shoulders. To do this, cast on a multiple of 4 sts plus 4, and work from the Bead Pattern Swatch Chart until you are comfortable with how the beads and sk2po decreases align – each bead should fall above a yarnover on the previous RS row and each sk2po should always be worked over a (k2tog, yo, k2tog) of the previous RS row.

Pattern

Back

Cast on 102 (110, 116, 122, 130, 136, 144, 150, 158) sts.
Row 1 (RS): [K1, p1] to end.
Rep row 1 for 2.5cm/1", ending with a WS row.
Next row (RS)(dec): K1, p1, sk2po, work in rib to last 4 sts, sk2po, p1. 4 sts dec **
Rep from ** to ** twice more. 90 (98, 104, 110, 118, 124, 132, 138, 146) sts
Rep row 1 until piece measures 9 (9, 9, 9, 9, 9.5, 9.5, 10, 10)cm/3½ (3½, 3½, 3½, 3½, 3¾, 3¾, 4, 4)" from cast-on edge, ending with a WS row.

Begin working in St st (knit RS rows, purl WS rows) and commence increases as follows:
Inc row (RS): K1, m1, k to last st, m1, k1. 2 sts inc
Next row (WS): P to end.

Continue in St st for a further 6 rows. Repeat Inc row on next row, then on every foll eighth row 4 (3, 3, 3, 3, 3, 3, 3, 2) times, then on every foll tenth row 2 (3, 3, 4, 3, 4, 3, 4, 4) times. 106 (114, 120, 128, 134, 142, 148, 156, 162) sts
Work straight without further increases until piece measures 26.5 (28, 28, 28, 29, 29, 29, 30.5, 30.5)cm/10½ (11, 11, 11, 11½, 11½, 11½, 12, 12)" or desired length from cast-on edge, ending with a WS row.

Shape armhole
Cast off 7 (8, 8, 11, 11, 13, 13, 13, 14) sts at beg of next 2 rows. 92 (98, 104, 106, 112, 116, 122, 130, 134) sts
Next row (RS): Ssk, k to last 2 sts, k2tog. 2 sts dec
Next row (WS): P2tog, p to last 2 sts, ssp. 2 sts dec
Working decreases as set by last two rows, dec 1 st at each end of every row a further 1 (3, 5, 5, 5, 5, 5, 7, 7) times then every RS row 1 (2, 2, 3, 3, 4, 4, 4, 4) times. 84 (84, 86, 86, 92, 94, 100, 104, 108) sts ***
Work straight until piece measures 16.5 (17, 18, 18.5, 19.5, 20.5, 21, 21.5, 22.5)cm/6½ (6¾, 7, 7¼, 7¾, 8, 8¼, 8½, 8¾)" from beginning of armhole shaping.

Shape neck
Next row (RS): K18 (18, 18, 18, 22, 22, 26, 26, 26) for right shoulder, cast off 48 (48, 50, 50, 48, 50, 48, 52, 56) sts for back neck, k to end.
Work each side of back neck separately. Place right shoulder sts on hold and continue to shape the left neck and shoulder as foll:
Row 1 (WS): P to last 2 sts, ssp. 1 st dec
Row 2 (RS): Ssk, k to end. 1 st dec
Row 3: P to end.
Rep rows 2–3 once, then rep row 2 only once more. 14 (14, 14, 14, 18, 18, 22, 22, 22) sts
Next row (WS): Cast off 5 (5, 5, 5, 6, 6, 7, 7, 7) sts, p to end.
Next row: K to end.
Next row: Cast off 5 (5, 5, 5, 6, 6, 7, 7, 7) sts, p to end.
Cast off remaining 4 (4, 4, 4, 6, 6, 8, 8, 8) sts.

Right neck and shoulder
With RS facing, rejoin yarn to right shoulder sts.
Row 1 (RS): K to last 2 sts, k2tog. 1 st dec
Row 2 (WS): P2tog, p to end. 1 st dec
Row 3: K to end.
Rep rows 2–3 once, then rep row 2 only once more. 14 (14, 14, 14, 18, 18, 22, 22, 22) sts
Next row (RS): Cast off 5 (5, 5, 5, 6, 6, 7, 7, 7) sts, k to end.
Next row: P to end.
Next row: Cast off 5 (5, 5, 5, 6, 6, 7, 7, 7) sts, k to end.
Cast off remaining 4 (4, 4, 4, 6, 6, 8, 8, 8) sts.

Front

Work as for back to *** and at the same time, when 10 (10, 10, 12, 12, 12, 12, 14, 14) rows of the armhole have been worked (not including the 2 armhole cast-off rows), ending with a WS row, establish Bead Pattern as follows (Note: for some sizes you will continue working armhole shaping as for back at the same time as establishing the Bead Pattern):
Place a locking stitch marker at the halfway point along the row (there should be an equal number of sts on each side of the marker).
Next row (RS): Patt to 2 sts before marker, working from chart or written Instructions work row 1 of Bead Pattern removing marker, patt to end.
Next row (WS): Patt to 1 st before first Bead Pattern decrease

of previous row, work row 2 of Bead Pattern, patt to end.

Next row (RS): Patt to 1 st before first Bead Pattern decrease of previous row, work row 3 of Bead Pattern, patt to end. Continue as set, working one less stitch before the next row of the Bead Pattern each time, until row 14 of Bead Pattern has been worked. Armhole shaping for all sizes should now be complete. 83 (83, 85, 85, 91, 93, 99, 103, 107) sts

Now continue to work one less stitch on each side as set, and rep rows 7–14 only of Bead Pattern a further three times, working 4-st repeat as many times as possible across patterned section.

Next row (RS): Continuing to expand the stitch pattern as set, patt as established until there are 20 (20, 21, 21, 24, 25, 28, 30, 32) sts on RH needle (ending with 'place bead'), k2, cast off 39 sts for front neck (1 st remains on RH needle from cast off), k1, patt as established (beginning with 'place bead') to end. 22 (22, 23, 23, 26, 27, 30, 32, 34) sts per shoulder

Note: Work each side of front neck separately. As you work the neck shaping, continue to expand the stitch pattern at the shoulder edge as set until all St st shoulder sts have been incorporated, then keep the Bead Pattern correct using the Bead Pattern Swatch Chart as a guide (*see* Pattern Notes) and only working a Bead Pattern increase/decrease if you can also work the corresponding decrease/increase. Otherwise, work edge stitches in St st.

Right neck

Row 1 (WS): Patt to last 3 sts, ssp, p1. 1 st dec

Row 2 (RS): K1, ssk, patt to end. 1 st dec

Dec 1 stitch at neck edge of every row a further 6 (6, 6, 6, 6, 6, 6, 8, 10) times, then every RS row 0 (0, 1, 1, 0, 1, 0, 0, 0) times. 14 (14, 14, 14, 18, 18, 22, 22, 22) sts

Work straight until piece measures 16.5 (17, 18, 18.5, 19.5, 20.5, 21, 21.5, 22.5)cm/6½ (6¾, 7, 7¼, 7¾, 8, 8¼, 8½, 8¾)" from beginning of underarm shaping, or matches back to shoulder, ending with an RS row.

Work as for back left shoulder.

Left neck

With WS facing, rejoin yarn to Left Neck stitches.

Row 1 (WS): P1, p2tog, patt to end. 1 st dec

Row 2 (RS): Patt to last 3 sts, k2tog, k1. 1 st dec

Dec 1 stitch at neck edge of every row a further 6 (6, 6, 6, 6,

6, 6, 8, 10) times, then every RS row 0 (0, 1, 1, 0, 1, 0, 0, 0) times. 14 (14, 14, 14, 18, 18, 22, 22, 22) sts

Work straight until piece measures 16.5 (17, 18, 18.5, 19.5, 20.5, 21, 21.5, 22.5)cm/6½ (6¾, 7, 7¼, 7¾, 8, 8¼, 8½, 8¾)" from beginning of underarm shaping, or matches back to shoulder, ending with a WS row.

Work as for back right shoulder.

Sleeves

Cast on 52 (54, 56, 60, 62, 64, 68, 74, 78) sts.

Row 1 (RS): [K1, p1] to end.

Rep row 1 for 5cm/2", ending with a WS row.

Change to larger needles.

Work 10 (10, 8, 8, 8, 4, 4, 4, 4) rows in St st, then commence increases:

Next row (Inc)(RS): K1, m1, k to last st, m1, k1. 2 sts inc

Continue in St st and repeat Inc row every foll eighth row 0 (0, 0, 2, 4, 5, 5, 5, 5) times, then every foll tenth row 0 (0, 3, 3, 3, 3, 2, 2, 2) times then every foll twelfth row 6 (6, 4, 3, 2, 2, 2, 2, 2) times. 66 (68, 72, 78, 82, 86, 88, 94, 98) sts

Work straight until piece measures 32 (32, 33, 33, 33, 34, 34, 34, 34)cm/12½ (12½, 13, 13, 13, 13½, 13½, 13½, 13½)" from cast-on edge, ending with a WS row.

Shape cap

Cast off 7 (8, 8, 11, 11, 13, 13, 13, 14) sts at beg of next 2 rows. 52 (52, 56, 56, 60, 60, 62, 68, 70) sts

Next row (RS): Ssk, k to last 2 sts, k2tog. 2 sts dec

Next row (WS): P2tog, p to last 2 sts, ssp. 2 sts dec

Working decreases as set by last two rows, dec 1 st at each end of: every row a further 1 (1, 1, 1, 1, 1, 1, 3, 3) times then every RS row 1 (1, 1, 1, 2, 2, 2, 3, 3) times, then every fourth row 8 (9, 9, 9, 9, 10, 10, 10, 10) times, then every RS row 5 (4, 5, 5, 5, 4, 4, 4, 4) times, then every row 3 times. 12 (12, 14, 14, 16, 16, 18, 18, 20) sts

Cast off 4 sts at beginning of next 2 rows. Cast off remaining 4 (4, 6, 6, 8, 8, 10, 10, 12) sts.

Neck edging

Sew the shoulder seams using backstitch.

Beginning at the left shoulder seam, evenly pick up and knit stitches around the entire neckline using the following ratio: approximately 3 sts for every 4 rows and 1 st for each cast-off st. The exact number of final stitches is not important.

Work an i-cord cast-off as foll:

Cast on 3 sts to left-hand needle, *k2, sl1 kwise, k1, psso, slip 3 sts on right-hand needle back to left-hand needle; rep from * until 3 sts remain, sl1, k2tog, psso. Fasten off leaving a long tail. Use the tail to neatly sew the gap closed.

Finishing

Sew side and sleeve seams using mattress stitch, then set in the sleeves using backstitch. Weave in all ends and block to measurements.

CHAPTER 14

BARBARA GLOVES

A pair of neatly fitting gloves was an important finishing touch to an outdoor outfit during this period. These delicately embellished gloves offer a chance to practise your embroidery skills on a small project that is pretty yet practical. Written for three hand sizes, the finger and wrist length can also easily be adjusted to fit your hand perfectly, with a buttoned opening allowing a close fit at the wrist.

Measurements
Sizes 1 (2, 3)
a. Circumference, at widest part of hand: 16 (17.5, 19)cm/6¼ (6¾, 7½)"
b. Length, wrist to middle finger tip: 23cm/9"
Length is easily varied to suit your hand size.

Materials
Stranded Dyeworks Oasis (4-ply/fingering weight; 75% Superwash Merino, 25% nylon; 424m/464yds per

Making it your own

- These gloves offer a blank canvas for your own creativity. Experiment with embroidered designs, or work a beaded stitch pattern across the wrist or the back of the hand.
- This pattern gives the gloves a picot folded hem, but this can easily be swapped out for a different hem (see Chapter 8). Alternatively, join to work in the round immediately after the cast-on and work a rib stitch in the round for an elastic cuff.
- For a different look, omit the button and button loop and leave the gap at the cuff open. Alternatively, use a needle and matching thread to sew a short length of ribbon to each side of the gap, and close the gap by tying a small bow instead.

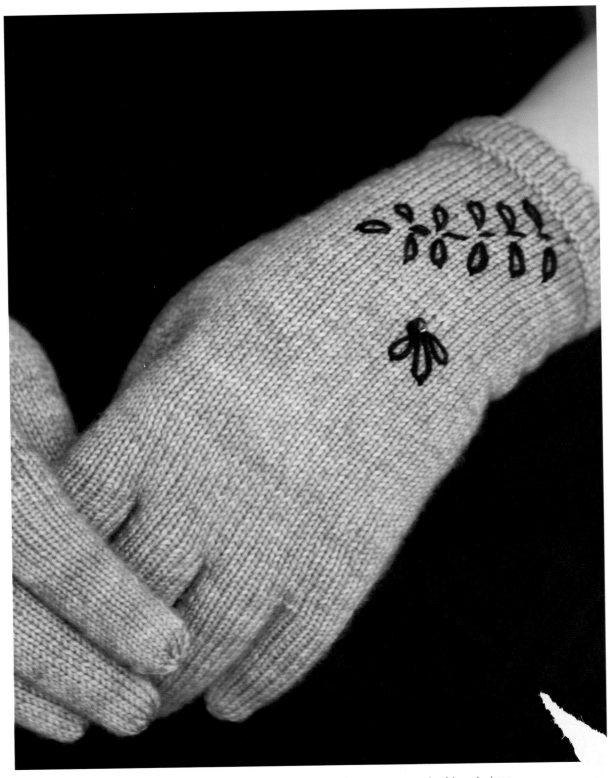

These gloves are the perfect blank slate for adding your own embroidery designs.

CHAPTER 18

BROOKS HAT

This intricately worked hat is inspired by the smart little berets that were popular throughout the 1920s and 30s. Beginning with a neat 1×1 twisted rib, it combines a variety of interesting techniques such as beading, diamond-shaped lace and purl motifs, and delicate columns of twisted knit stitches. The beret shape is encouraged by blocking it carefully over a plate during the finishing process, but for a more modern, close-fitting beanie style it can simply be blocked flat instead.

Measurements
Measurements are taken after firm blocking into flat beret shape.

One size

a. Circumference at widest point: 66cm/26"

b. Total length (cast-on edge to crown): 18cm/7"

Brooks features intricate lace, beaded and twisted stitches, for a hat that's as fun to knit as it is to wear.

Making it your own

As this is a small project, achieving an exact tension is not important, so the stitch patterns used can be adjusted. Try the following modifications for a unique look:

- **Remove the lace pattern** Keep the focus on the purl diamond texture by removing the lace pattern – on rows 1, 3, 5 and 7, omit the beads and work M1 in place of the yarnovers. Throughout the rest of the chart, omit the beads, yarnovers and lace pattern decreases, working those stitches as plain knit stitches and working only the crown shaping decreases marked in blue on the chart.

- **Remove all patterns** For a plain hat, remove all the patterns by completing the ribbed brim, then knitting for 40 rounds. Alternatively, keep some interest at the brim by working the first 14 rows of the chart as described in the lace-free version above, then knitting for 26 rows. Work the crown shaping decreases following rows 41–61 of the chart, working all sts apart from those marked in blue as plain knit stitches. Work all of the shaping decreases knitwise throughout, replacing p2tog with k2tog and ssp with ssk.

- **Add your own patterns** Working a plain beret as above offers a wide variety of possibilities – try working a beaded pattern around the hat by completing the ribbed brim, knitting a couple of plain rounds, then working Floral Trim, Beaded Diamonds, or your chosen beaded pattern. Work this pattern once above the brim or repeat it up the entire 40 rounds to the beginning of the crown shaping. Alternatively, keep the beret plain during the knitting, then use it as a blank slate for embroidery afterwards. Remember to block the hat into the desired shape before embroidering, to avoid distorting the stitches.

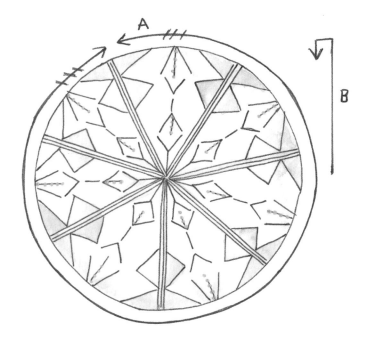

Brooks schematic.

Needles

Note: Preferred method of working in the round may be used, such as DPNs, a 40cm/16" circular needle, or a long circular needle and the magic loop method.

2.25mm/US 0 knitting needles suitable for working in the round

2.75mm/US 2 knitting needles suitable for working in the round

Tapestry needle

Gauge

32 sts & 49 rows to 10cm/4", measured over 1×1 twisted rib with 2.75mm needles, after blocking and stretched flat

Matching gauge exactly is not essential for this project.

Materials

BC Garn Silkbloom Fino (4-ply/fingering; 55% merino wool, 45% mulberry silk; 200m/220yds per 50g/1¾oz ball)

Shade: IX14; 1 ball

91 size 6 seed beads

Special stitches

Place bead (pb): Work to the stitch to be beaded, place bead on crochet hook then place stitch on hook. Draw the bead down the hook and onto the stitch; return beaded stitch to left needle and knit it (*see* Chapter 6 for tutorial).

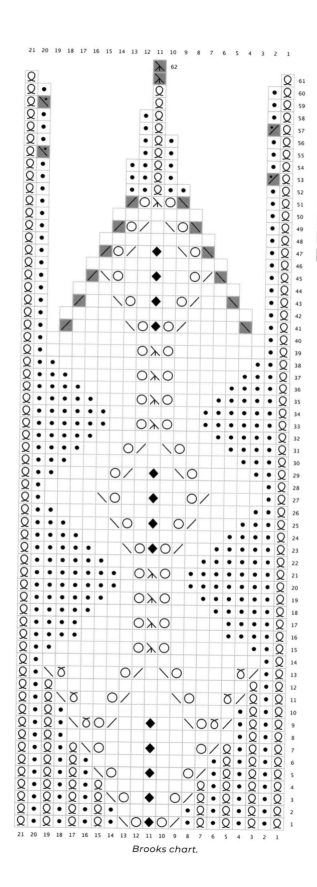

Brooks chart.

Written instructions for chart

Round 1: [K1tbl, p1] 4 times, k2tog, yo, pb, yo, ssk, [p1, k1tbl] 4 times. 21 sts

Round 2: [K1tbl, p11] 4 times, k5, [p1, k1tbl] 4 times.

Round 3: [K1tbl, p1] 3 times, k1tbl, k2tog, yo, k1, pb, k1, yo, ssk, [k1tbl, p1] 3 times, k1tbl.

Round 4: [K1tbl, p1] 3 times, k1tbl, k7, [k1tbl, p1] 3 times, k1tbl.

Round 5: [K1tbl, p1] 3 times, k2tog, yo, k2, pb, k2, yo, ssk, [p1, k1tbl] 3 times.

Round 6: [K1tbl, p1] 3 times, k9, [p1, k1tbl] 3 times.

Round 7: [K1tbl, p1] twice, k1tbl, k2tog, yo, k3, pb, k3, yo, ssk, [k1tbl, p1] twice, k1tbl.

Round 8: [K1tbl, p1) twice, k13, [p1, k1tbl] twice.

Round 9: [K1tbl, p1] twice, k2tog, m1, yo, ssk, k2, pb, k2, k2tog, yo, m1, ssk, [p1, k1tbl] twice.

Round 10: Rep round 8.

Round 11: K1tbl, p1, k1tbl, k2tog, m1, k2, yo, ssk, k3, k2tog, yo, k2, m1, ssk, k1tbl, p1, k1tbl.

Round 12: K1tbl, p1, k1tbl, k15, k1tbl, p1, k1tbl.

Round 13: K1tbl, p1, k2tog, m1, k4, yo, ssk, k1, k2tog, yo, k4, m1, ssk, p1, k1tbl.

Round 14: K1tbl, p1, k17, p1, k1tbl.

Round 15: K1tbl, p2, k6, yo, sk2po, yo, k6, p2, k1tbl.

Round 16: K1tbl, p4, k11, p5.

Round 17: K1tbl, p4, k4, yo, sk2po, yo, k4, p4, k1tbl.

Round 18: K1tbl, p5, k9, p5, k1tbl.

Round 19: K1tbl, p6, k2, yo, sk2po, yo, k2, p6, k1tbl.

Round 20: K1tbl, p7, k5, p7, k1tbl.

Round 21: K1tbl, p7, k1, yo, sk2po, yo, k1, p7, k1tbl.

Round 22: K1tbl, p6, k7, p6, k1tbl.

Round 23: K1tbl, p5, k2, k2tog, yo, pb, yo, ssk, k2, p5, k1tbl.

Round 24: K1tbl, p4, k11, p4, k1tbl.

Round 25: K1tbl, p3, k3, k2tog, yo, k1, pb, k1, yo, ssk, k3, p3, k1tbl.

Round 26: K1tbl, p2, k15, p2, k1tbl.

Round 27: K1tbl, p1, k4, k2tog, yo, k2, pb, k2, yo, ssk, k4, p1, k1tbl.

Round 28: Rep round 14.

Round 29: K1tbl, p2, k4, yo, ssk, k1, pb, k1, k2tog, yo, k4, p2, k1tbl.

Round 30: K1tbl, p3, k13, p3, k1tbl.

Round 31: K1tbl, p4, k3, yo, ssk, k1, k2tog, yo, k3, p4, k1tbl.

Round 32: Rep round 18.

Round 33: Rep round 19.

Round 34: Rep round 22.

Round 35: K1tbl, p5, k3, yo, sk2po, yo, k3, p5, k1tbl.
Round 36: Rep round 24.
Round 37: K1tbl, p3, k5, yo, sk2po, yo, k5, p3, k1tbl.
Round 38: Rep round 26.
Round 39: K1tbl, p1, k7, yo, sk2po, yo, k7, p1, k1tbl.
Round 40: Rep round 14.
Round 41: K1tbl, p1, ssk, k4, k2tog, yo, pb, yo, ssk, k4, k2tog, p1, k1tbl. 19 sts
Round 42: K1tbl, p1, k15, p1, k1tbl.
Round 43: K1tbl, p1, ssk, k2, k2tog, yo, k1, pb, k1, yo, ssk, k2, k2tog, p1, k1tbl. 17 sts
Round 44: K1tbl, p1, k13, p1, k1tbl.
Round 45: K1tbl, p1, ssk, k2tog, yo, k2, pb, k2, yo, ssk, k2tog, p1, k1tbl. 15 sts
Round 46: K1tbl, p1, k11, p1, k1tbl.
Round 47: K1tbl, p1, ssk, yo, ssk, k1, pb, k1, k2tog, yo, k2tog, p1, k1tbl. 13 sts
Round 48: K1tbl, p1, k9, p1, k1tbl.
Round 49: K1tbl, p1, ssk, yo, ssk, k1, k2tog, yo, k2tog, p1, k1tbl. 11 sts
Round 50: K1tbl, p1, k7, p1, k1tbl.
Round 51: K1tbl, p1, ssk, yo, sk2po, yo, k2tog, p1, k1tbl. 9 sts
Round 52: [K1tbl, p3] twice, k1tbl.
Round 53: K1tbl, p2tog, p1, k1tbl, p3, k1tbl. 8 sts
Round 54: K1tbl, p2, k1tbl, p3, k1tbl.
Round 55: K1tbl, p2, k1tbl, p, ssp, k1tbl. 7 sts
Round 56: [K1tbl, p2] twice, k1tbl.
Round 57: K1tbl, p2tog, k1tbl, p2, k1tbl. 6 sts
Round 58: K1tbl, p1, k1tbl, p2, k1tbl.
Round 59: K1tbl, p1, k1tbl, ssp, k1tbl. 5 sts
Round 60: [K1tbl, p1] twice, k1tbl.
Round 61: K1tbl, sk2po, k1tbl. 3 sts
Round 62: Sk2po. 1 st

Pattern

Ribbed Brim

Using smaller needles, cast on 147 sts. PM and join to work in the round.
Round 1: *[K1tbl, p1] 10 times, k1tbl; rep from * to end.
Rep round 1 until piece measures 4cm/1½" from cast-on edge.

Hat

Change to larger needles and begin working from chart as follows:
Round 1: Work row 1 of chart, working 21-st rep 7 times across the round.
Continue to work through the chart as set until all 62 rows have been worked. 7 sts
Cut yarn, leaving a long yarn end. Thread the yarn through the remaining sts and pull tight to close.

Finishing
Weave in all ends. Block firmly to open up the lace, preferably over a medium-sized plate to encourage a flat beret shape.

ABBREVIATIONS

beg	Beginning
dec	Decrease
foll	Follow(s)/Following
inc	Increase
k	Knit
kwise	Knitwise (as though to knit)
kfb	Knit into the front and back of a stitch
k2tog	Knit two stitches together
LH	Left-hand
M1	Work as M1L
M1L	With left needle tip pick up strand between needles from front to back and knit into the back of this stitch
M1R	With left needle tip pick up strand between needles from back to front and knit into the front of this stitch
M1P	Pick up strand between the two needles from front to back with the tip of left needle, purl into the back of this stitch
patt	Pattern
PM	Place marker
p	Purl
pwise	Purlwise (as though to purl)
pb	Place bead
pfb	Purl into the front and back of a stitch
pbf	Purl into the back then front of a stitch
p2tog	Purl two stitches together
p3tog	Purl three stitches together
rem	Remain(s)/remaining
rep	Repeat
rev St st	Reverse stocking stitch (stockinette): purl on RS rows, knit on WS rows
RH	Right hand
RS	Right side
sl	Slip
s2kpo	Slip two stitches together knitwise, knit next stitch, pass slipped stitches over
sk2po	Slip one stitch knitwise, knit next two stitches together, pass slipped stitch over
ssk	Slip two stitches knitwise one at a time, knit together through the back loops
ssp	Slip two stitches knitwise one at a time, purl together through the back loops
sssk	Slip three stitches knitwise one at a time, knit together through the back loops
sssp	Slip three stitches knitwise one at a time, purl together through the back loops
SM	Slip marker
st(s)	Stitch(es)
St st	Stocking stitch/stockinette (worked flat: knit RS rows, purl WS rows; worked in the round: knit every round)
tbl	Through the back loop
tog	Together
wyib	With yarn held at back of work
wyif	With yarn held at front of work
WS	Wrong side
yo	Yarn over needle and into correct working position for next stitch

Cable Stitches:

1/1/1 RPC	Slip 2 sts to cable needle and hold at back of work, k1, slip 1 st from cable needle back to left needle, p1, k1 from cable needle.
1/1/1 RPT	Slip 2 sts to cable needle and hold at back of work, k1tbl, slip 1 st from cable needle back to left needle, p1, k1tbl from cable needle.
2/1/2 RPC	Slip 3 sts to cable needle and hold at back of work, k2, slip 1 st from cable needle back to left needle, p1, k2 from cable needle.

2/2/2 RPC	Slip 4 sts to cable needle and hold at back of work, k2, slip 2 sts from cable needle back to left needle, p2, k2 from cable needle.
1/1 LC	Slip 1 st to cable needle and hold at front of work, k1, k1 from cable needle.
1/1 RC	Slip 1 st to cable needle and hold at back of work, k1, k1 from cable needle.
1/1 LPC	Slip 1 st to cable needle and hold at front of work, p1, k1 from cable needle.
1/1 RPC	Slip 1 st to cable needle and hold at back of work, k1, p1 from cable needle.
1/1 LPT	Slip 1 st to cable needle and hold at front of work, p1, k1tbl from cable needle.
1/1 RPT	Slip 1 st to cable needle and hold at back of work, k1tbl, p1 from cable needle.
1/2 RC	Slip 2 sts to cable needle and hold at back of work, k1, k2 from cable needle.
1/2 LC	Slip 1 st to cable needle and hold at front of work, k2, k1 from cable needle.
1/2 RPC	Slip 2 sts to cable needle and hold at back of work, k1, p2 from cable needle.

1/2 LPC	Slip 1 st to cable needle and hold at front of work, p2, k1 from cable needle.
2/1 RPC	Slip 1 st to cable needle and hold at back of work, k2, p1 from cable needle.
2/1 LPC	Slip 2 sts to cable needle and hold at front of work, p1, k2 from cable needle.
2/2 RC	Slip 2 sts to cable needle and hold at back of work, k2, k2 from cable needle.
2/2 LC	Slip 2 sts to cable needle and hold at front of work, k2, k2 from cable needle.
2/2 RPC	Slip 2 sts to cable needle and hold at back of work, k2, p2 from cable needle.
2/2 LPC	Slip 2 sts to cable needle and hold at front of work, p2, k2 from cable needle.
3/3 RC	Slip 3 sts to cable needle and hold at back of work, k3, k3 from cable needle.
3/3 LC	Slip 3 sts to cable needle and hold at front of work, k3, k3 from cable needle.
5/5 LC	Slip 5 sts to cable needle and hold at front of work, k5, k5 from cable needle.
5/5 RC	Slip 5 sts to cable needle and hold at back of work, k5, k5 from cable needle.

RESOURCES AND FURTHER READING

From period fashion sourcebooks, to inspiring stitch dictionaries, to vintage knitwear patterns, these resources provide a wealth of inspiration for building a vintage hand-knit wardrobe.

Vintage Fashion and Design

Fashion Sourcebook: 1920s and *Fashion Sourcebook: 1930s* (Goodman-Fiell, 2016)
Edited by Charlotte Fiell & Emmanuelle Dirix
These sourcebooks are packed with original photographs and illustrations from the period, making them an indispensable resource for anyone interested in vintage fashion.

Art Deco: 1910–1939 (V&A, 2015)
Edited by Charlotte Benton, Tim Benton and Ghislaine Wood
An in-depth look at the design movement behind the fashion.

1920s Jazz Age: Fashion & Photographs (Unicorn, 2016)
By Martin Pel
A detailed look at the fashions, designers and photographers of the Jazz Age.

Knitting Resources

The Knitter's Book of Yarn (Potter Craft, 2007)
By Clara Parkes
A comprehensive look at yarns, fibres, and choosing the best yarn for your projects.

Japanese Knitting Stitch Bible: 260 Exquisite Patterns by Hitomi Shida (Tuttle Publishing, 2017)
By Hitomi Shida
Translated by Gayle Roehm
If intricate patterning makes your heart sing, this stitch dictionary is for you. Many of the delicate stitch patterns included in this book fit perfectly into an Art Deco aesthetic.

The Principles of Knitting (Touchstone, 2012)
By June Hemmons Hiatt
This impressive book covers every aspect of knitting technique, so it's a great resource to keep on your bookshelf.

Websites

www.ravelry.com
The home for knitters on the internet, with a database searchable by every attribute imaginable, Ravelry is the best place to find those modern patterns with a vintage flair.
www.antiquepatternlibrary.org
A catalogue of scanned antique and vintage patterns for many different crafts, including knitting and crochet.
www.youtube.com
YouTube is the perfect place to find technique tutorials if you learn best by following a video.

Vintage Knitwear

A Stitch in Time, Volume 1 (Arbour House Publishing, 2008) and *Volume 2* (Arbour House Publishing, 2011)

By Susan Crawford & Jane Waller
These beautiful books feature original vintage patterns reworked and updated for the modern knitter.

The Vintage Shetland Project (Susan Crawford Vintage, 2018)
By Susan Crawford
Colourwork is a huge topic that was beyond the scope of this book, but it has an important role in vintage fashion. This book gives an incredibly in-depth look at Shetland colourwork in the first half of the twentieth century, with patterns recreated from original vintage pieces.

Materials Source List

Beautiful knitwear starts with beautiful yarn. Here's where to find the yarns used in this book.

BC Garn
Yarn: Silkbloom Fino
www.loveknitting.com

Debonnaire Yarns
Yarn: Squeal Lace
www.debonnaireyarns.com

Fyberspates
Yarn: Scrumptious 4 Ply/Sport Superwash
www.fyberspates.com

John Arbon Textiles
Yarn: Devonia
www.jarbon.com

Kettle Yarn Co.
Yarn: Beyul Fingering
www.kettleyarnco.co.uk

Quince & Co
Yarns: Finch and Tern
www.quinceandco.com
UK stockists: **www.loopknitting.com**

Stranded Dyeworks
Yarn: Oasis
www.strandeddyeworks.com

West Yorkshire Spinners
Yarn: Exquisite
www.wyspinners.com

INDEX